BEHAVIOR
THERAPY
IN
PSYCHIATRY

BEHAVIOR THERAPY IN PSYCHIATRY

JASON ARONSON

A Report of the American Psychiatric Association Task Force on Behavior Therapy

New York

First Aronson edition 1974

LIBRARY OF CONGRESS CATALOGING IN PUBLICATION DATA

APA Task Force on Behavior Therapy
  Behavior therapy in psychiatry.

  Reprint of the 1973 ed. published by the American
Psychiatric Association, Washington, as its Task force
report 5.
  1. Behavior therapy. I. Title. II. Series:
American Psychiatric Association. Task force report 5.
RC489.B4A18 1974   616.8'914   74–3227
ISBN 0–87668–139–9

Manufactured in the United States of America

The American Psychiatric Association
Task Force on Behavior Therapy

Lee Birk, M.D. Chairman
Stephanie B. Stolz, Ph.D.
John Paul Brady, M.D.
Joseph V. Brady, Ph.D.
Arnold A. Lazarus, Ph.D.
James J. Lynch, Ph.D.
Alan J. Rosenthal, M.D.
W. Douglas Skelton, M.D.
Joseph B. Stevens, M.D.
Edwin J. Thomas, Ph.D.

CONTENTS

CONTENTS

CONTENTS

[x]

PREFATORY
NOTE

The American Psychiatric Association Task Force on Behavior Therapy was established to study the historical development of behavior therapy, its efficacy for the treatment of psychiatric problems, its current forms and uses as well as potential abuses, and its relationship to dynamic psychiatry. The Task Force was also asked to make recommendations for medical student education and residency training, and to point out areas needing further research. Behavioral treatment has grown considerably in the last few years, yet medical students enter psychiatric training with only minimal information about learning principles, and behavior therapy is poorly represented in the departments of psychiatry. Both dynamic psychiatrists and behavior therapists were members of the Task Force. We hope that our combined report will provide further impetus for mutually beneficial interactions between dynamic psychiatrists and behavior therapists.

[xiii]

PREFATORY NOTE

The authors thank George W. Albee, Ph.D.; John Cameron, m.b., ch.b.; Jack R. Ewalt, M.D.; C. B. Ferster, Ph.D.; Seymour S. Kety, M.D.; Judd Marmor, M.D.; John McFarlane Rhoads, M.D.; Joseph Wolpe, M.D., for their helpful suggestions; Mr. Jason Saffer and Ann Brinkley, Ph.D. for their editorial assistance; and Ms. Beverly Rubin for her care in preparing the bibliographic references.

INTRODUCTION

The term *behavior therapy*, and the roughly synonymous terms *behavior modification* and *conditioning therapy*, first appeared in the psychiatric and psychological literature around twenty years ago. It is now part of the active vocabulary of virtually all psychiatrists and clinical psychologists in the United States and is known to most educated laymen as well. The rapid growth of interest in this approach is evident from the clinical literature. Figure 1 shows the rate of growth in the number of articles on behavior therapy that appeared in four major psychiatric and psychological journals from 1951 to 1970. The marked increase suggested by these curves is all the more striking when one considers that four new journals devoted entirely to behavior therapy were begun during the last eight years of the period shown. *Behavior Research and Therapy* was started in 1963, the *Journal of Applied Behavior Analysis* in 1968, and *Behavior Therapy* and the *Journal of Behavior Therapy and Experimental Psychiatry* in 1970. During 1970, the last year shown in Figure 1, these four journals published 182 articles on behavior therapy. Textbooks, monographs, and published symposia devoted to behavior therapy have also been appearing with increasing frequency.

Of course, this current popularity does not establish the value of a behavioral approach or insure lasting interest, both of which depend on empirical demonstrations of effectiveness. One section of this report, therefore, is concerned with evidence for the efficacy of behavior therapy.

Despite the number of clinical and research papers already published on behavior therapy, and its coverage in the general medical and lay press, those actively involved in the field are frequently asked very basic questions about behavior therapy by colleagues in psychiatry and psychology, as well as by non-psychiatrist physicians and persons in other counseling professions. "What is behavior therapy?" "How did it originate?" "What is it good for?" "What is the evidence for its efficacy?" One also hears (or overhears) casual or at times rather emotional statements about behavior therapy that indicate large areas of misunderstanding and mistrust. Examples are: the beliefs that behavior therapy works best (or only) with the nonverbal or unintelligent patient, is synonymous with hypnotherapy, is applicable mainly to phobias and other "discrete" conditions, is practiced only by psychologists, usually entails electric shock or other aversive stimuli, and always involves the manipulation of an unwilling patient. All these are false.

The purpose of this report is to inform the reader of the nature and origin of behavior therapy and to clarify some basic issues related to its methodology and range of application. We also hope to stimulate the reader to learn more about this clinical approach to psychiatry through independent reading, participation in courses, conferences, and symposia, and especially through an ongoing reevaluation of the clinical data encountered in his own practice.

The last section of this report is a condensed technical overview of some basic behavioral principles. Although this section may be difficult and slow going, we feel it is necessary. Just as one needs some understanding of chemistry to be a good physician, one needs some technical grounding in the basic concepts and principles of learning in order to understand what behavior therapy is really about.

The increasing interest in and concern with behavior therapy bear undeniable witness to its presence on the American psychiatric scene, and suggests the need for an interim review of its origins, scope, and efficacy. While this necessarily brief report cannot do justice to the broad spectrum of behavioral treatment approaches currently being used and developed, we hope it will nonetheless serve to explicate and clarify some basic conceptual and methodological issues. In addition, we hope the report will encourage further research, the development of behavior therapy training programs, and continuing inquiry by the individual psychiatrist.

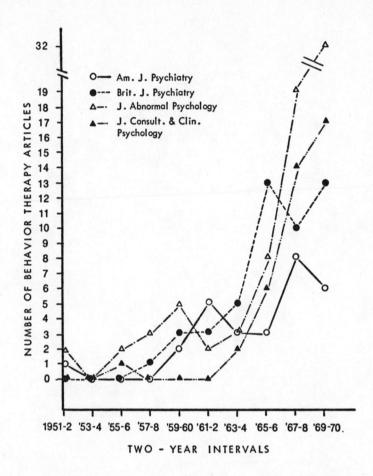

Fig. 1. The number of articles on behavior therapy that appeared in four major journals in the last 20 years. (Reprinted by permission from Brady, J. P. "Behavior Therapy: Fad or Psychotherapy of the Future?" in *Advances in Behavior Therapy, 1970,* edited by Rubin, R. D., Henderson, J. D., Pumroy, D. K., et al, Academic Press, New York, 1972.)

HISTORY
AND
DEFINITIONS

The nature and origins of behavior therapy are perhaps best revealed in answers to the following questions: What is behavior therapy? What are the conditions under which it emerged? While it seems unlikely that these questions can be easily answered in a manner that will satisfy both the clinically oriented therapist and the research oriented theoretician, it may be useful to delineate the subject matter of behavior therapy and describe its historical roots insofar as these appear relevant to the development of current treatment practices.

Definition of Behavior Therapy

IN the most general sense, the subject matter of behavior therapy focuses on the modification of interactions between person and environment. More specifically, it emphasizes the systematic application of experimentally derived behavior-analysis principles to effect observable and, at least in principle, measurable changes in this interaction process. Behavior therapy is most appropriately defined in operational terms, by describing what behavior therapists actually do in analyzing a patient's problems, specifying treatment objectives, arranging treatment conditions, and evaluating treatment outcomes.

The behavior therapist begins with a detailed and objective description of the patient's problem behavior. In the empirical tradition of the laboratory from which the approach is derived, the focus of this functional analysis is on observable and quantifiable behavior, rather than on inferred unconscious conflicts. In developing this analysis, the therapist looks for particular situations in which the behavior typically occurs or fails to occur, as well as for current maintaining conditions.

The second distinguishing characteristic of be-

[2]

havioral approaches to clinical problems concerns the focus or objective of the treatment that is developed on the basis of this initial functional analysis, Here again, emphasis is placed on modification of the principal presenting symptoms, rather than on analysis or understanding of the character structure or unconscious conflicts presumed to underlie the behavior pattern.

Third, the behavior therapy treatment program, conceptualized in terms of experimentally derived learning principles, focuses on systematic manipulation of the environmental and behavioral variables thought to be functionally related to the disturbing performance. Fourth, because behavior therapy has this experimental-clinical tradition, the therapist tries, whenever possible, to assess treatment outcomes in the same objective, quantifiable terms that characterized both the initial problem analysis and the formulation of the treatment program. The behavior therapist prefers to assess treatment effects by observing and recording behavior, rather than by getting scores on paper and pencil tests. Performance changes are the objective criteria that either validate the initial tentative analysis, or require a re-examination of this analysis to include, if necessary, the collection of additional data.

History of
Behavior Therapy

THE origins of behavior therapy are found in the laboratory animal learning and conditioning studies of Pavlov (1, 2) and Bechterev (3) in the Soviet Union, and Thorndike (4) in the United States. These early investigations provided the first systematic basis for conceptualizing the behavioral interactions between organism and environment within the framework of an orderly and self-consistent body of scientific knowledge based on observation and experiment. Virtually all forms of behavior therapy have been derived more or less directly from the foundations of conditioned reflex (Pavlovian) studies and operant conditioning (Skinnerian) research on learning.

The distinctive manner in which the behavior therapist approaches a functional analysis of presenting symptoms in relation to the observable aspects of antecedent events and currently maintaining environmental conditions, can be seen to have much in common with the experimental approach to the analysis of behavior. Indeed, the objective recording and quantification of clinical data in the evaluation of adjustment problems and specification of treatment goals repre-

[4]

sent procedures that adhere closely to the methodology characteristic of the laboratory foundations of behavior therapy.

Early behavioral research

As the section on basic concepts (pp. 119–135) reflects, the range of basic science studies underlying behavior therapy extends well beyond reflex conditioning. Included in the scientific roots of behavior therapy are many sophisticated studies of verbal behavior (5), cognitive learning (6) and modeling (7).

Several streams of development intervened between the emerging "behaviorism" of Russian and American experimental psychology early in the century, and the current applications of behavior analysis procedures in the treatment of human adjustment problems. During the 1920's and 1930's, for example, the writings of Watson and Rayner (8), Jones (9), and Mowrer and Mowrer (10), among others in the United States, were indicative of the trend toward using learning and conditioning principles in approaching various problem behaviors in both educational and clinical settings. In the same era, Soviet psychophysiologists (11, 12), adhering closely to conceptualizations derived directly from laboratory research, became increasingly involved in psychological treatment and, by the 1940's, the experimental work of Gantt (13), Liddell (14), and Masserman (15) had begun to establish a laboratory base for Pavlovian psychiatry (16) in America.

Systematic attempts to reformulate psychoanalytic treatment practices in learning theory terms appeared in academic psychology by the mid-1940's. The work of Shoben (17), Mowrer (18), and Dollard and Miller (19), among others, set the stage for the development and rapid expansion of behavior therapy in the 1950's and 1960's.

Later developments

Current applications of behavior analysis methods have emerged over the past twenty years principally as the result of three somewhat independent developments on three continents. These derive from the work of Wolpe and his associates begun in South Africa, from the work at Maudsley Hospital in London, and from the work identified with American applied operant conditioners. These three influences emerged independently but almost simultaneously, and provided refinements that have now begun to coalesce in the development of behavior therapy as a systematic and comprehensive clinical treatment approach.

The clinical and experimental innovations of Wolpe

and his colleagues Lazarus and Rachman in South Africa during the early 1950's (20) were based in part on laboratory research within the framework of Hullian learning theory, a theory based on Pavlov's conditioned reflex notions. Starting with an analysis of the role of conditioned emotional responses in the acquisition and maintenance of maladaptive behavior patterns in laboratory experiments with cats, Wolpe (21) developed and extended the Sherringtonian principle of reciprocal inhibition to encompass counteracting response effects on anxiety-evoking stimulus bonds. He extrapolated these generally neurophysiological concepts to the human neuroses, and introduced systematic desensitization procedures that stressed classical conditioning effects involving the identification of symptom-eliciting antecedent stimulus events and respondent extinction of neurotic patterns. The subsequent move by Wolpe and Lazarus to the United States, and Rachman's decision to join the group at Maudsley Hospital in England not only provided the occasion for dispersal of these early conditioning therapy developments but also facilitated the interchange of ideas, techniques, and applications with other approaches.

A second source of direct influence in the development of behavior therapy was a group of psychologists and psychiatrists in London around 1950 who were following Eysenck's and Shapiro's lead in attempting to bridge what they perceived to be a distressingly wide gap between laboratory-based learning principles and clinically-oriented psychotherapeutic practices. Emphasizing experimental analysis and hypothesis-testing in individual case studies (22, 23, 24), this basically empirical approach to clinical assessment proved readily adaptable to treatment situations. Systematic attempts to change maladaptive behavior by carrying out controlled experiments in the clinic resulted in a focus on explicit operational descriptions of the psychiatric entity.

The third major impetus to the application of behavior analysis principles to clinical treatment emerged in the United States during the 1950's based on the earlier work of Skinner (25). This innovative experimental approach to behavior emphasized the study of the individual interacting with the environment, and focused attention on the effects or consequences of operant or "voluntary" performances as the principal determinant of behavior. Unlike other approaches prominent in American psychology, which was preoccupied at the time with the average behavior of groups of persons, Skinner and his students (notably Ferster, Lindsley, and Azrin, among others) emphasized the control of behavior in the individual as a basis for behavioral science.

The earliest operant experimental studies of psychotics were reported by Lindsley and Skinner (26) and by Ferster and DeMyer (27). These laboratory studies showed that the behavior of severely disturbed persons was subject to the same learning principles as that of normal persons. In 1961 Ayllon and Azrin (28, 29), working with chronic adult psychotics, began to develop the ward management procedures that have come to be known as the token economy. Operant treatment programs for mildly disturbed preschool children and retardates were begun at this same time by Wolf, Baer, and their collaborators (30, 31, 32).

Over the past decade, a broad range of applications within the operant conditioning framework has extended behavior modification procedures to numerous individual and institutional settings, both clinical and educational (33). Although work with children continues to be emphasized, the precise measurement techniques and careful arrangement of environmental contingencies characteristic of the operant approach have produced reliable behavioral change in a variety of target populations.

Past relationship of behavior therapy and dynamic psychiatry

Dynamic psychiatry and behavior therapy have grown up separately out of completely different traditions. Dynamic psychiatry emphasizes helping people understand and deal with their feelings. This approach evolved through the efforts of clinicians (mostly physicians) to help troubled patients. As practiced in the United States, it derives its theoretical framework largely from the ideas of Freud, Hartmann, Meyer, Sullivan, and Franz Alexander. Behavior therapy, as we have noted, has developed more or less systematically from theory and experiments by psychologists, much of the basic research having been done by experimental psychologists working with nonhuman animals. At its best, behavior therapy tries to remain firmly rooted in experimental data.

Especially in the last decade, these two streams in American psychiatry have been progressively converging, but the convergence has been regrettably slow. It is likely that a synergistic cooperation has been slow to develop between the two traditions probably mainly because very few people are well trained and experienced in both. This has led both behavior therapists and dynamic psychiatrists to hold naive conceptions of the other's position. Salzman (34), Marmor (35) and other psychoanalysts have appropriately criticized behavior therapists for their attack in the 1970's on the psychoanalytic thinking of the 1920's, and behavior therapists (36) have similarly criticized analysts for attacking in the 1970's the straw man of the oversimplified view of the early strict behaviorists of the 1920's.

Other appropriate criticisms have been made. For example, behavior therapists and some philosophers of science accuse analytically oriented therapists of failing to collect data relevant to their theories or even to document whether their treatments work, and of failing to frame testable hypotheses (37). Psychoanalytic orthodoxy, with its reliance on libido theory and Freud's tripartite mental apparatus with its allegorical entities, id, ego, and superego, has been heavily criticized, not only by Skinner (38) and other behaviorists (39), but also by Rado (40), Bieber (41), Marmor (42) and others (43, 44, 45, 46). On the other hand, dynamic psychiatrists have appropriately criticized behavior therapists for at times knowing very little about the clinical syndromes in which they are intervening or the patients they are attempting to treat. Psychiatrists also criticize behavior therapists for tending to be ignorant and nihilistic about psychotherapy at its best and blind to its subtleties, while simultaneously being rather insular. On the whole, both behavior therapists and dynamic psychiatrists seem to have been unwilling to inform themselves sufficiently to be able to consider the observations presented by the other approach.

In recent years, however, some behavior therapists and dynamic therapists, many of the latter analysts, have felt there is value in incorporating the best of both traditions, the clinical and the experimental, into practical psychiatry (47, 48, 49, 50). As evidence of that rapproachement, several behavior therapist-psychoanalyst teams now work together cooperatively and synergistically in a clinical association.

Thus, agreement is emerging among some persons that there are areas of overlap between the traditions of dynamic psychiatry and behavior therapy. These clinicians believe that it would be irresponsible to reject out of hand beneficial and workable approaches, from whatever school they are derived. Later in this report (see pp. 86–89), we will cite a few examples of areas of mutual interest and concern where there exists an especially clear potential for combining and using the experience of both traditions.

BEHAVIOR
THERAPY
METHODS

Behavior therapy as an applied clinical discipline involves two related steps: conducting an analysis of the adjustment problems presented by the patient and carrying out a program of treatment. The first of these, the behavioral analysis, is the more difficult of the two, requiring much clinical experience and sophistication, and a considerable knowledge of the environmental determinants of behavior. If the analysis is in error or incomplete, a successful treatment outcome is unlikely. The behavioral analysis makes use of both the methods and the results of experimental behavioral science. Indeed, what distinguishes a behavioral approach from alternative clinical approaches is its reliance on a natural science model.

The analysis typically begins with a detailed behavioral description of those day-to-day performances that cause distress or interfere with optimal functioning of the individual in familial, social, vocational, or other important spheres of activity. The target behaviors are viewed in the context of the patient's entire repertoire of responses, and also in relation to the sorts of consequences his environment is capable of providing over the long term.

This description, whenever possible, is based on observation of the patient in the setting in which he reports he is distressed. These observations may be careful quantitative records or statements about the relative frequency of various behaviors. The person making the observations may be the therapist or his agent, a peer of the patient, or the patient himself. These empirical observations are often supplemented by the patient's description of how he thinks or feels (e.g., he may report anxiety, guilt, distressing fantasies), how he performs at current important life tasks (e.g., failure to go to work, failure in school assignments), or how he interacts with others (e.g., abusive behavior toward his children, withdrawn and uncommunicative behavior with the opposite sex). Information is also obtained by direct observation or from the patient's report on areas of his life in which he functions adequately or optimally, since these assets are part of the total evaluation of the patient and are useful in planning a program of treatment. A preliminary analysis is made before formal treatment begins, and the behavioral analysis is continually modified and refined as more is learned about the patient and his environment from his responses to ongoing events, including the treatment itself.

What are usually termed "symptoms" in psychiatry are analyzed in terms of their observable behavioral components. Thus psychiatric disorders are described in terms of behavior that may be totally lacking, infrequent, or weak in intensity, excessive, or occurring under inappropriate circumstances. It is important also that the description be quantitative. This is almost always possible, at least at the level of a frequency count. Thus, a parent can be trained to tally the frequency with which a child stutters, a teacher or hospital aide can keep a record of a child's aggressive outbursts, and a well motivated patient can count the frequency of his intrusive obsessional thoughts.

In addition to this topographical description of what the patient does and does not do, the behavior therapist does a functional analysis to find how the behavior relates to organismic and environmental variables. Here the behavioral clinician examines both the antecedents and the consequences of the problematic behavior, to determine the circumstances under which the disordered behavior seems to occur, and the environmental consequences that might be maintaining the behavior. In this sort of behavioral assessment, the individuality of each patient is explicitly recognized, and the therapeutic procedures are tailored to the individual case.

After doing a behavioral analysis, the clinician is in a position to formulate clinical hypotheses about the origin and maintenance of the patient's current maladaptive state. In so doing, he makes use of general principles of conditioning and learning, as well as his observations of previous patients and their social environments in the hospital, clinic, and natural ecological setting. Behavior therapy permits the testing of such clinical hypotheses by the systematic manipulation of behavioral and environmental variables thought to be functionally related to the patient's difficulties. However, the primary goal of behavior therapy is the modification of behavior.

In this section, we include brief descriptions of those behavior therapy methods most commonly used. This is a young field, and other techniques are currently being developed and evaluated by clinical researchers. Thus the ones we include here should not be considered an exhaustive list.

Systematic Desensitization

GRADUAL progressive exposure to feared situations has long been advocated as a means of eliminating or reducing maladaptive anxiety and avoidance behavior; in systematic desensitization the exposure is pre-planned, and in graduated steps. A classic report of this procedure (9) described how a phobic child, during a period of hunger, was given something to eat while the feared object was slowly brought nearer to the child. Care was taken to keep the phobic stimulus at a sufficient distance so as not to interfere with the child's eating. As the phobic object was slowly brought nearer, the child's tolerance increased, and he was soon able to touch it without alarm, whether or not food was forthcoming.

Description of systematic desensitization therapy

Wolpe (21) developed systematic desensitization, a coherent, theoretically based approach for treating anxiety. His work led to the wide adoption of the proce-

[17]

dures of systematic desensitization. According to Wolpe, if a response antagonistic to anxiety can be made to occur in the presence of anxiety-evoking stimuli, so that the stimuli are accompanied by a complete or partial suppression of the anxiety response, the bond between these stimuli and the anxiety will be weakened. He says that mere exposure to feared situations is unlikely to extinguish the fear unless responses that will compete with the anxiety response are simultaneously elicited.

One of the first applications of this approach in a clinical setting was reported by Salter (51), who had used it in treating a claustrophobic patient. Salter trained the patient to relax when feeling claustrophobic. In this case, desensitization was applied in the absence of the actual feared object or situation, with the therapist relying exclusively on the patient's imagination, plus relaxation and counterphobic sensations.

Systematic desensitization (21) approaches the treatment of specific anxiety responses by ordering the patient's fears in a hierarchy, with relatively small gradations between successive fear items. Thus, a typical hierarchy of scenes for deconditioning maladaptive anxiety in the treatment of sexual inhibition (frigidity) would be:

1. Being kissed on lips by husband
2. Same as above but with tongue contact
3. Breasts fondled while fully clothed
4. Undressing with husband in bedroom

[18]

5. Being kissed on lips while nude
6. Seeing husband with erection
7. Fondling of breasts while nude
8. Mouth contact with breasts by husband
9. Nude in bed with husband preparatory to coitus
10. As above with initial body contact
11. As above with kissing on lips and breast fondling
12. As above immediately before intromission
13. Intromission
14. Continuing coitus (ventral-ventral) (52)

While such hierarchies of the patient's significant fears and hypersensitivities are being constructed, the patient goes through an accelerated version of Jacobson's (53) progressive relaxation training sequence. After the patient learns the relaxation technique, desensitization proper commences with the deeply relaxed patient being asked to imagine the least disturbing item. Even the slightest degree of tension or discomfort must be eliminated before successive items in the hierarchy are presented. The patient is asked to signal if scenes prove disturbing, whereupon they are immediately withdrawn, relaxation is reinstituted, and the imagined scene is presented again and again (or in a "diluted" form) until the patient can report continued relaxation. If the patient in the clinical setting can picture the most subjectively distressing scene without reporting anxiety, usually he will also report successful transfer to the real life situation.

[19]

Applicability of
systematic desensitization

Since the early experimentation with individual and group desensitization (54, 55, 56), there has been a striking surge of interest in this clinical technique. A voluminous literature on systematic desensitization now exists, including case reports, experimental studies, monographs, and reviews.

The clinical reports describe the use of systematic desensitization on a wide variety of cases and problem areas far transcending monosymptomatic phobias. For example, there are reports of the successful use of systematic desensitization for frigidity (57), insomnia (58), and exhibitionism (59). Reports have also appeared in which short-acting barbiturates, used in place of relaxation, tended to hasten desensitization in the treatment of frigidity and anxiety (52, 60). Desensitization techniques have been adapted for use with children with phobic or avoidance behavior disorders (61). These techniques for children use pleasurable story telling and imagery rather than relaxation to compete with anxiety-producing stimuli.

Research on
systematic desensitization

The many experimental reports have been mainly concerned with identifying the active ingredients of the desensitization procedure. To what extent is it a method of counter-conditioning rather than extinction? How vital is the relaxation training? To what extent does the patient improve because he expects to improve? How much attention needs to be applied to the calibration of the hierarchies? The foregoing suggest the sort of critical issues being evaluated in laboratory settings. Several thorough reviews of this extensive literature have been published so far (62, 63, 64). In our opinion the clinical issues of major importance are the indications and contra-indications. This is important because systematic desensitization can be mechanically applied, and some feel that it has on occasion been used with patients who would have responded far better to a program that included chemotherapy, as in schizophrenic syndromes (65).

The advantages of systematic desensitization are that the therapeutic target can be clearly defined and delimited, and changes in the person's response can be measured psychophysiologically as well as behaviorally. Also, the method is sufficiently precise to allow computerized application (66). The practicing therapist will probably find that although the technique is tedious, it

[21]

has the advantage of being relatively straightforward and useful as a therapeutic technique for dealing with anxiety, especially anxiety that is triggered by identifiable stimuli.

Token Economies and Operant Principles in Ward Management

APPLICATION of the principles and procedures of operant conditioning to psychiatric treatment programs, including ward or group management situations, has been multiplying in almost geometric proportion over the last fifteen years. Ayllon and Azrin and their colleagues (28, 29, 67, 68) have given a major impetus to the use of operant principles in ward management. These programs have used various procedures such as positive reinforcement to develop and maintain appropriate behaviors and the removal of positive reinforcement to decrease the frequency of inappropriate behavior.

A number of studies have shown that many patients tend to engage in the behavior that the nurses and ward aides pay attention to (69, 70); that is, for these patients, social interaction with the nurses and aides is reinforcing. However, attention and concern from staff does not always reinforce patients' behavior. In addition, items generally considered rewarding, such as money or cigarettes, are reinforcers for some, but not for everyone. The problem in developing a successful ward management program based on operant methods is to find a reinforcer of wide applicability, one that can follow immediately the behavior it is designed to reinforce. Laboratory research suggests that such a reinforcer would have maximum clinical effectiveness. One solution is to use a conditioned reinforcer, a token, to bridge the delay between the occurrence of the desired response and the availability of the reinforcing stimulus, and to provide a money-like currency that can then be exchanged for a variety of items and activities, according to the patient's choice (29). Some suitable conditioned reinforcers are points, credits, money, and checks, which can be chosen according to the effective functioning level of a particular patient population.

The token economy system is unlike many ward management systems that tend to encourage patient dependency (71). It is basically a work-payment incentive system. As such, it strengthens behaviors compatible with those in the society at large, such as regular performance on a job, self-care, maintenance of one's living quarters, and exchange of currency for desired items. To have a successful token economy program, the staff must specify the desired behaviors, develop a currency system that includes some kind of token to be dispensed by staff and exchanged by patients, and provide an adequate array of positively reinforcing consequences that can be obtained as the result of token exchange.

Operant principles employed via token economies are powerful agents of behavior change. Of perhaps as great importance is the fact that non-professional personnel are the actual agents of therapeutic change in a token system. Professional manpower is limited. If therapeutic procedures are going to be extended to the many persons who require help, professional personnel must make increased use of those who are in direct contact with the patient, such as nurses, aides, correctional officers, friends and family members.

Applicability of the token economy system

The early development of the token economy system took place almost exclusively within the context of the closed ward psychiatric treatment center and was found quite useful in preventing or overcoming the habit deterioration or social breakdown syndrome that accompanies prolonged custodial hospitalization, whatever the initial diagnosis. The operant principles involved are now being extended to acute psychiatric programs having an average patient stay of days to weeks. These programs use reinforcers that are available in the hospital (e.g., visiting privileges and telephone use), and teach the staff how to avoid reinforcing and hence perpetuating abnormal behavior.

Token procedures are in use in a wide range of other settings as well. They have been widely adopted in the public school classroom, and also are being used in classrooms with disadvantaged, hyperactive, retarded, and emotionally disturbed children (72, 73). Such programs have also been used with delinquents and persons with character disorders to enhance educational achievement and to improve adjustment to military or civilian environments (74, 75, 76). Tokens have been used to increase children's attention span and improve self-help skills in retardates (77, 78). These treatment procedures are often used in conjunction with individual, group, and pharmacologic therapies. There is no inherent difficulty in this, as long as objectives are clearly stated for each approach and for the combined approaches.

The goal of any treatment is the amelioration of the patient's difficulties with the improvement continuing after the termination of therapy. The ideal token program would include a specification of the environment to which the patients must ultimately return, such as a halfway facility or the community at large, and would include provision for establishing and strengthening behavior useful in that environment (76). Token reinforcement systems have already been demonstrably successful in improving performance within the institution (28), improving patient socialization, reducing extreme or bizarre behavior, and facilitating instrumental role performance in chronically institutionalized mental hospital populations (71). However, the token system's influence in facilitating return of the chronic patient to society is just beginning to be evaluated.

An explicit intermediate step or steps between the therapeutic system and the natural environment facilitates generalization. Often various levels or steps are built into a program, and the individual must progress through these before returning to the natural environment. The first level is usually a standard token economy system designed to improve self-care and behavior on the ward. The second level might involve token reinforcement for off-ward jobs, and educational or vocational training. The higher levels often provide other sources of positive reinforcement such as private rooms, increased privileges, longer passes, and the opportunity to participate in the management of the program. The final level may be residence in the community where all or most of the reinforcement comes from the natural environment through pay checks, raises, promotions, and praise. Colman (76) has demonstrated the success of a token reinforcement treatment program using such a scaled format in significantly improving the way soldiers with character disorders adjusted to the army.

A few reservations about the use of token economies

Patients' responses to token systems vary, even when the ward management procedure is properly established. With chronic schizophrenic populations, it is not unusual to find that approximately ten percent of the patients are essentially non-responsive in that they do not engage in any of the behaviors for which they may receive tokens (28). Further research may suggest changes in the procedures that would result in these non-responsive patients also interacting with the system.

When a token economy is in effect, relatively few

patients will have their behavior accelerated tremendously in all of the areas for which they may earn tokens. More commonly, because of the many choices patients have concerning what they may do to earn tokens, some behaviors will show marked change while others will not necessarily be changed greatly, even though it is possible to earn tokens in connection with them. This is also a technical defect that could presumably be remedied by specifically designed and individualized contingencies of reinforcement. For example, a patient who habitually earns tokens to the point of satiation by making his bed and keeping his room straight, but who never engages in conversation with other patients, could be helped beyond this impasse by gradually changing him over to a progressively attenuated reinforcement schedule for bed making, while socializing behaviors are consistently reinforced.

Recently there has been increasing concern with the so-called artificiality of token systems (79), particularly when reinforcers are used that are not likely to be found in the natural environment to which the patient may return (80). However, if other methods have failed to teach a patient skills he will need to lead a normal life, tokens can have a priming function, enabling him to acquire a satisfactory performance of some desired behavior. Once the newly learned skill is well established, generalization to other situations will be facilitated if the patient is gradually shifted to more natural consequences, that is, to those events that would follow the new behavior in the real world. Generalization to the natural environment and progressive switching from arbitrary to natural reinforcement are areas that require further exploration and development.

Aversive Control: Aversion Therapy amd Punishment Techniques

SOME types of inappropriate behavior appear to be maintained because their natural consequences are reinforcing for the individual, such as addictions and sexual attractions to inappropriate stimuli. Aversive control techniques are often included in behavior therapists' repertoires of treatment for these and other inappropriate behaviors having long-term consequences detrimental to the patient.

[29]

Learning principles
underlying aversive control

The use of stimuli that are unpleasant to the patient can be conceptualized in two different ways, depending on the relationship of the target behavior and the stimuli coming before and after that behavior.

In the classical conditioning or Pavlovian approach, the behavior therapist pairs an aversive stimulus with a stimulus that precedes the undesirable behavior. For example, if a behavior therapist were attempting to treat alcoholism by giving a patient an emetic, the look, smell, and taste of various alcoholic beverages would be associated with the drug-induced nausea. The goal of this treatment is to have the patient experience nausea, vomiting, and general malaise when in the presence of alcoholic beverages and thus presumably avoid drinking such beverages.

On the other hand, in the operant conditioning approach, the aversive control procedure would be to follow specific responses with an aversive stimulus. In the alcoholism example, the patient might be given an electric shock just as he begins to drink an alcoholic beverage. In this case, the goal of treatment is to reduce markedly the probability of occurrence of a drinking response.

Although these two procedures can be differentially defined operationally and conceptually, in practice each procedure often will contain components of the other, so that the designation of a procedure as operant conditioning or classical conditioning is, in many instances, arbitrary.

Aversion therapy

One of the earliest reports of the classical conditioning use of aversive control was by Max (81), who described the diminution of a patient's homosexual fixation after receiving electric shocks. Also relatively early was Raymond's (82) account of treatment of a fetishist by apomorphine conditioning. More recently examples have appeared in the literature which illustrate the progressive technical refinement of aversive control methods in the treatment of sexual deviations (83, 84, 85), and the melding of such techniques with a dynamic clinical approach (86).

During the forties many reports appeared on the use of emetic drugs, especially for teaching alcoholics abstinence (87), but this early work was seriously hampered by poor control of the timing of the punishing stimulus as is inherent in the method of using emetic drugs, unlike shock, and by insufficient clinical attention to the need for combining such techniques with other therapy aimed at developing suitable coping behaviors. More recent research on alcoholism has employed precisely timed shock as a punishing stimulus and

[31]

precisely defined behaviors, like continued drinking beyond a criterion blood alcohol level. This has reportedly been successful in many cases in helping problem drinkers to achieve a level of moderate social drinking (88).

Punishment techniques

Aversive control conceptualized in operant conditioning terms involves two quite different procedures: first, the addition of an aversive stimulus after the inappropriate behavior, and second, the removal of a positive stimulus after the inappropriate behavior.

It is the first of these—punishment—that most people think of when "aversive control" is mentioned. The presentation of aversive stimuli following an undesirable response has been used in behavior therapy primarily to control self-injurious and self-destructive behavior such as head-banging or tongue-biting. The evidence indicates that such behavior can be eliminated with a brief application of a strong aversive stimulus immediately after the response (89, 90). Such a procedure should be accompanied by withdrawal of any social reinforcement for the self-destructive behavior, and positive reinforcement of responses that would compete with self-destruction.

An alternative method, also based on learning principles, for eliminating self-destructive behavior would be to use only withdrawal of social reinforcement, rather than withdrawal combined with punishment. This approach is unwise in many cases, however, because a large body of research has shown that the initial reaction to the withdrawal of reinforcement that has been previously given for a response is an increase in the frequency of that response (91). Because of the life-threatening nature of some self-destructive behavior, withdrawal of social reinforcement should not be the only procedure used.

The second operant conditioning method of aversive control described above is the removal of positive reinforcement, such as a loss of privileges following a given behavior. This is a technique commonly used by American parents (92). Laboratory results have shown that the effects of the removal of positive reinforcement are analogous to the effects of adding an aversive stimulus following a response, with the possibility that the removal of positive reinforcement might have much weaker emotional effects (93).

With either of these operant aversive control techniques, as long as the patient does not perform the undesirable behavior, the punishment does not occur, that is, he is able to avoid being punished. Avoidance of punishment thus is one way to conceptualize the effects of a threat, in which the therapist specifies an unpleasant event that will occur if the patient performs an undesired behavior. For example, a therapist might say, "If you break windows or take off your clothes, you will be restricted to your room," or, "So long as you don't break windows or take off your clothes, you won't be restricted to your room and can have ward privileges." In learning theory terms, the threat functions as a discriminative stimulus, indicating to the patient the conditions under which the aversive contingency would be put into effect.

Contrast of avoidance technique with contingency contracting

Control by threat is in sharp contrast to a contingency contract in which the therapist specifies a reinforcing event that will occur if a patient performs a desired behavior. For example, the therapist might say, "If your room is neat and you are properly groomed, you can go to the movies."

This seemingly subtle distinction is actually an important one because of what we learn in our culture about methods of control. Culturally, aversive control in any form, including threats, is considered to be punishing and a restriction of freedom. That is, aversive control is itself aversive, even if the person threatened successfully avoids the actual carrying out of the threat so that he is never punished. In contrast, control by positive means is generally considered "normal," is culturally acceptable and is considered to be compatible with freedom. For example, we do not feel that it is inappropriate or restrictive to receive a salary for a period of working on a job, even though this is in fact a contingency contract between the employer and the employee.

Efficacy of punishment techniques

A consistent finding from research on aversive control is that the effects of the therapeutic punishment seem to be restricted to the particular behavior that is punished, in that particular situation, with that particular therapist. That is, the effects of punishment as a therapeutic procedure in behavior therapy seem to generalize very little (89, 91).

In contrast to the somewhat limited effects of punishment on the target behavior, the positive side effects of this treatment seem to be rather widespread. For example, the common report in the literature is that once punishment has eliminated a patient's self-injurous behavior, he avoids people less, and is more responsive to other therapy aimed at his learning adaptive responses (91).

On the whole, the results reported suggest that punishment and aversion therapy are effective techniques when used in combination with other proce-

[35]

dures (91, 93, 94). The most effective way to eliminate inappropriate behavior appears to be to punish it while at the same time reinforcing the desired behavior (95).

Punishment leads to response suppression and not, as in extinction, to response elimination (25). Although the predicted and observed corollary is that the effects of aversion therapy are only temporary (95, 96, 97), the patient at least for a time will not make the undesirable response. During that time, he is more amenable to learning new appropriate responses. If the environment then supports these new responses, the effects of the aversive control will be lasting. The behavior therapist should keep in mind, however, that in the absence of rewarded alternatives, the suppressed response will recur. To ensure that the previously eliminated response does not recur, the patient should be taught behavior that will be maintained by natural rewards in the environment. Because there is sometimes a lag in the process of learning new behaviors, the therapist must, if necessary, also be prepared to use additional aversive control in the form of occasional "booster" conditioning sessions (91).

Assertive training

WHEN a person fails to stand up for his rights in a firm and dominant (not aggressive and domineering) manner, he may not have acquired appropriate assertive behaviors, and may have learned maladaptive fear or rage reactions that inhibit assertive responses. Habitually meek persons as well as persons who typically over-react to real or imagined slights from others by expressing inappropriate rage are appropriate candidates for assertive training. Persons who are inhibited in the expression of positive feelings may also be considered for a kind of assertive training; this subtype of assertive training is sometimes called "training in emotional freedom" (98).

Truly effective assertive responses are unlikely in the face of high anxiety, so some patients may require desensitization to facilitate assertive training.

Although assertive training is generally considered one of the major behavior therapy procedures, there is still a regrettable lack of systematic research in this area. Nevertheless, it is easy to find successful histories of a wide range of cases treated in a variety of settings, providing suggestive evidence for the efficacy of the approach. From a research point of view, one difficulty is that often other methods like psychotherapy are employed in addition to assertive training.

[37]

Although assertive behavior is difficult to define, there seems to be general agreement that assertive behavior is an interpersonal response involving a frank, honest, and direct expression of ongoing feelings. According to some authorities, the therapeutic impact of an assertive response is a result of the assumed incompatibility between anger and anxiety. After the patient learns to make negative statements of annoyance, irritation, or disgust, or positive statements of praise and affection, any attendant anxieties will be inhibited by this expressive behavior. At present, psychophysiological evidence of an inhibition of anxiety is far from clear (99). The most observable change following assertive therapy is the alteration in interpersonal interaction.

Description of assertive training

A prerequisite for assertive training is that the behavioral analysis should have shown that the patient's problem involves inappropriate responses such as timid, withdrawn, submissive and other socially inhibited behaviors, or belligerence, rages, and aggressive acting out. The adverse consequences of these maladaptive behaviors are then specifically documented for the patient, while differences between assertive and aggressive behaviors are emphasized.

Successful case histories are presented to encourage the patient's active participation. A general instigation to more assertive behavior is backed up by more specific behavior rehearsal, including role reversal. In behavior rehearsal, the therapist assumes the role of significant others in the patient's life, and a series of increasingly exacting scenes are enacted within the protective confines of the consulting room. During rehearsal procedures, the therapist monitors the patient's verbal content, his mode of expression, tone of voice, inflection, and resonance. The therapist uses feedback, with or without tape recorded sequences, in a behavioral-shaping, role-playing paradigm which eventually enables the patient to remove apologetic hesitations or querulous overtones. Nonverbal behavior, such as posture, gait, eye contact, and facial expression, is also modified.

When patient and therapist feel that punitive consequences are unlikely to follow the patient's real life efforts, he is encouraged to try out his new skills outside of the therapy hour. Whenever possible, precautions are taken to ensure that feedback from the environment will be supportive and positively reinforcing. Additional refinement of the patient's assertive skills is achieved by having him keep notes of his interpersonal failures and successes, and each performance is assessed in detail. It seems that the most useful assertive response is one in which the patient is taught not just to express displeasure, but also to provide information that would facilitate a more acceptable interaction. ("I wish you wouldn't yell at me. If you approached me more gently, I would make fewer mistakes." "It really gets me mad when you use curse words like that. If you stop trying to put me down, I might be able to listen to your request.")

These procedures are amenable to group meetings as well as individual therapy (100). In fact, groups often permit a wider range of role playing situations (101, 102) and facilitate generalization to the real life situation (103).

Childhood behavior disorders such as extreme withdrawal, isolation, inhibition, or passivity may also be treated with assertive training techniques. Therapeutic methods that involve modeling plus reinforcement of the appropriate behavior in the natural environment can be considered assertive training techniques. These procedures have been much more carefully evaluated experimentally than the clinical assertive therapy described above. Reinforcement of children's appropriate assertive behavior by therapists, parents and teachers has proved successful in reducing or eliminating behavior such as withdrawal (31). Modeling of more assertive behavior can also be done effectively by parents and teachers (104). Role playing, behavior rehearsal, and reinforcement in group settings are other techniques that can be used with older children and adolescents.

[40]

Although clinical impressions suggest that there is probably a fair degree of transfer and generalization from one assertive encounter to another, this point lacks experimental documentation. With some cases, gains seem to be situation-specific. The use of Ellis's rational emotive psychotherapy (105) may facilitate therapeutic transfer and generalization (98). In this type of therapy, the patient is taught to use rational "self talk" to undermine the fears or impotent rage reactions that inhibit assertive responses.

Flooding

FLOODING, like systematic desensitization, is a procedure for the removal of maladaptive anxiety, although the indications for its use are less frequent than for systematic desensitization. It is based on the observation that irrational fears leading to avoidance behavior may be overcome by having the patient confront the

[41]

anxiety-arousing situation at a high level of intensity for prolonged periods of time.

Description of flooding

This procedure, related to a laboratory technique of preventing an avoidance response, usually called response prevention (106), has come into use only very recently, and it is conducted differently by different investigators. Typically, however, the patient is confronted with anxiety-provoking cues either in imagination or in real life for long periods of time. For example, if he has a fear of heights and goes to great lengths to avoid high places, he might be instructed to imagine as vividly as possible that he is on the roof of a tall building, looking down at the ground through a guard rail. Such a patient will probably manifest intense anxiety while either experiencing or imagining such a scene, but the anxiety tends to diminish to an easily tolerable level after 5 to 20 minutes. On the next trial, preferably within a few days of the first, the initial anxiety tends to be less, and less time is therefore required for a state of calm to be attained.

Usually the fear and the associated phobic avoidance behavior extinguish after several trials. Some patients require a much longer exposure on each trial before the anxiety decreases substantially. When flooding is used, it is important to avoid terminating the scene and its associated anxiety before the patient has reached a state of relative equanimity. Premature removal of an anxiety-generating scene is tantamount to an escape trial, and would tend to reinforce fear conditioning and avoidance behavior.

Efficacy of flooding

The efficacy of flooding for the removal of phobias is not yet well established by adequately controlled clinical studies. Also, there is some disagreement in the literature as to the relative efficacy of flooding and systematic desensitization (107, 108). Some claim has been made that, in general, *in vivo* procedures tend to work better than imagined procedures (109). Additional clinical research is needed in this area. Flooding carries some risk, since it entails provoking intense anxiety in the patient, and a judgment needs to be made in each case as to whether intense anxiety can be experienced safely by the patient, and whether the discomfort and the risk are justified by the potential benefits.

[43]

Miscellaneous Behavioral Techniques

WHILE most of the behavior therapy procedures we have described are derived from or based on principles of learning, other behavioral techniques are largely of empirical origin, derived from the observation of clinical phenomena and their relation to environmental events. They qualify as behavioral techniques insofar as their further development, refinement and validation entails the systematic, controlled study of the interaction of the behavior to be modified and the variables manipulated in the treatment. We will briefly describe two quite different procedures as examples.

Metronome-conditioned speech retraining

This procedure was developed for the treatment of severe stuttering (110). Clinically, it has been observed that most stutterers show a marked and usually immediate increase in fluency if they pace their speech with the rhythmic beats of an auditory metronome.

Although this phenomenon has been known for many years (111), it was little used in the treatment of stuttering because the fluency obtained by the stutterer when using a desk metronome in the clinician's office carried over poorly to other speaking situations unaided by a metronome, especially those fraught with anticipatory anxiety and tension. This problem proved to be soluble, however, by virtue of the development of a miniaturized metronome that could be worn unobtrusively by the patient on his person, usually behind the ear like a hearing aid, thus enabling him to pace his speech in ordinary speaking situations (112). Systematic experimental studies of the effects of metronomes of different rates, sensory modalities, and so on, led to the design of instruments with characteristics optimal for retraining the speech habits of stutterers (113, 114).

In addition, principles of learning were used in the design of a retraining program (113). In brief, the program begins by finding conditions under which the patient can be highly fluent in a low stress situation, such as reading to the therapist or to a close friend. With a severe stutterer, this may mean having the patient pace one syllable of his speech to each beat of a metronome set as slow as 40 beats per minute. Then the patient learns to increase his rate of speech gradually as the metronome is speeded up; he also learns to pace larger units of speech to each metronomic signal. At the same time, the situations in which he is using the device are extended systematically from speaking with only the therapist or with one other person to using the device for more complex, anxiety-arousing speaking occasions. When the patient has a high degree of fluency in most speaking situations, he begins to discontinue the use of the device in the same systematic fashion, first discontinuing the use of the metronome in the easiest, least stressful situations, then in the next least stressful and so forth. The initial clinical trials with this procedure are promising (110).

Negative practice

Negative practice, sometimes called paradoxical intention, is another procedure that has no clear basis in learning principles, though there are some theories about this (115). It has been used principally in the treatment of high frequency repetitive behavior. In this method, the patient is told to repeat the symptomatic behavior deliberately during the treatment sessions. In the cases of tics, the patient might purposefully demonstrate his typical tic behavior several thousand times in the course of a thirty-minute massed practice session. For maximum therapeutic effect, the patient might have five to ten such sessions each week. Between sessions, the patients appear to tic much less frequently. Treatment is terminated when the frequency of tics has dropped to zero or to an acceptable level. Moderately good results have been obtained in the treatment of some tiqueurs by negative practice. Although the technique does not work for all tic patients, it has been successfully used with some patients in whom the tic was part of a *Gilles de la Tourette's* syndrome (115, 116).

MISCONCEPTIONS
ABOUT
BEHAVIOR
THERAPY

Any new technique that promises to be powerful in the modification of human behavior raises a number of questions. This section of the report discusses some common concerns about behavior therapy.

The Concern that Behavior Therapy is Coercive, Manipulative, and Controlling

WHEN psychoanalytic theory was first introduced, it raised the spectre of unethical authoritarian control. In like manner, some critics of behavior therapy contend that the behavioral approach is coercive, manipulative, controlling, potentially even machiavellian, and that it thus poses broad social dangers.

While it is true that there are moral and ethical issues attending the use of behavior therapy, these issues are not unique to that approach. The same problems must be faced by all therapeutic approaches. In discussing the moral aspects of behavioral control, Bandura states:

> . . . It is essential to recognize that social influence is not a question of imposing controls where none existed before. All behavior is inevitably controlled. . . . The process of behavior change, therefore, involves substituting new controlling conditions for those that have regulated a person's behavior. The moral question is not whether man's behavior will be controlled, but rather by whom, by what means, and for what ends (93).

Behavior is always controlled, though the influences may be various. A therapeutic encounter is no exception.

The ethical issue of control faces all therapists, whether or not they acknowledge it. Even the nondirective and evocative therapies involve intentional as well as unwitting influence (117). Therapists guide interviews and therapeutic transactions, if only by being passive; almost all therapeutic endeavors involve the socialization of patients in the practices of that therapy; almost all psychotherapeutic encounters entail some differential reinforcement of the patient by the therapist through verbal and nonverbal cues; many therapists put themselves in the position of judging what is undesirable, sick or inappropriate, and what is desirable, healthy and appropriate.

Behavior therapists tend to face the issue of control more directly than do some psychotherapists. Behavior therapists tend to engage in influences that are overt, explicit and planned, whereas many psychotherapists exercise influences that are covert, implicit and unplanned (118). The behavior therapist tends to work mainly on contracted problem areas, with clinical goals that necessarily involve the specification of which behavior is slated to change if the technique is successful, In contrast, many psychotherapists are less strict in focusing their own and the patient's attention only on behaviors mutually recognized as a problem.

Part of the fear of behavioral techniques as manipulative seems to arise out of the fact that when the behavioral techniques are effective, they can be quite powerful indeed, and may work with striking rapidity. This is unlike what occurs, for example, during even a highly successful psychoanalysis in which very striking and pervasive changes in behavior may also occur, but where these changes generally develop gradually over three, four, five or more years.

The Concern That Symptom Substitution Will Occur

A second common misconception about behavior therapy is that because it addresses only symptoms and not the underlying causes, the basic problems remain untreated, with the consequence that symptom sub-stitution will occur.

First, formulations about overt behavior that attribute it to unobserved and unobservable mental complexes are not strategically useful to behaviorists. Behavior therapists have observed that cognitive changes are neither necessary nor sufficient prior conditions for changes in action. Cognitive changes (insights) may catalyze behavioral changes (actions), as in successful psychotherapy, but, as both experienced psychotherapists and behavior therapists can testify, it is often the other way around, that is, insight develops after successful behavior change (93, 119).

Second, to the extent that a given problem behavior is a prominent part of the patient's repertoire, is frequently emitted and is the source of reinforcement for him, a reduction of this behavior will both allow more opportunity for other behavior to occur and result in a loss of reinforcement. Appropriately designed therapy should anticipate this and, as part of the therapeutic program, teach the patient new, desirable behavior.

For example, if an alcoholic who formerly drank heavily stops drinking, he will lose whatever reinforcers he got from drinking, such as anxiety reduction and avoidance of a home situation. In addition, he will have more time available to devote to other activities. A well designed behavioral approach to alcoholism would include not only a procedure to stop the alcoholic from drinking, but also a therapeutic procedure such as desensitization or assertive training to deal with the patient's entire situation. Similarly, if it appears that a child's maladaptive behavior is maintained by attention from his parents, a well designed behavior therapy program for that family would not only teach the parents to ignore the problem behavior, but also show them how to interact with their child in such a way as to support new and mutually reinforcing appropriate behavior.

Third, every endeavor by a behavior therapist to alter problem behavior would be an invitation for symptom substitution to occur if this idea were correct. That is, if symptom substitution were likely to occur, behavior therapists should have encountered innumerable instances of it when successfully changing behavior. The literature of both dynamic psychiatry and of behavior therapy rebuts this idea, however, because while there is a large number of reports of successful behavior therapy, there are few references to the emergence of maladaptive substitute responses.

For example, an extensive review of studies using behavioral techniques for the control of nocturnal enuresis showed that successful treatment of the enuresis did not produce adverse personality changes or other symptom substitution (115, 120). Careful analyses of the results of other behavior therapy methods with a wide variety of problems have also failed to reveal any evidence for symptom substitution (63, 121). In fact, several studies (122, 123) have reported that when the specific behavior being treated responded to the therapy, other inappropriate behavior decreased; untreated appropriate behavior also improved, as did verbal attitudes (93). Because there are occasional instances in which adverse changes do follow behavior therapy, and especially because of the instances in which favorable side-effects occur, much more needs to be known about behavior changes that are correlated with treatment.

In conclusion, the whole problem of symptom substitution can be understood best by remembering that problem or deviant behavior is approached analytically by the behavior therapist with the goal of understanding what processes of conditioning were involved in the acquisition of the maladaptive response and what reinforcement is maintaining it. Maladaptive responses obey the same laws of learning and conditioning as do so-called normal responses and are thus amenable to alteration through the careful application of learning and behavior modification principles.

The Concern That Behavior Therapists Rely on Punitive Measures

SOME clinicians think that behavior therapists depend largely on punishment and that they indiscriminately apply aversive techniques. As a matter of fact, many behavior therapists use few if any aversive techniques. Competent behavior therapists who do use them do so selectively and with a strong emphasis on the practical necessity for combining aversive techniques, when they are used, with positive techniques that are capable of increasing desirable behaviors that can compete successfully with problem behaviors.

The Concern That Behavior Therapists Ignore Subjective Experience

ANOTHER concern is that behavior therapists deny the existence of subjective events and thus overlook the patient's subjective life—his feelings and fantasies. This is simply not true, although there is a marked disinclination among behaviorists to work with such private responses because of the obvious difficulties they pose in terms of observation and measurement. However, behavior therapists agree that private events like fantasies are real events for the individual experiencing them. Although they cannot be experienced directly by an outside observer, such events are subject to indirect observation and crude measurement.

To the extent that observation and measurement can be introduced, behaviorists are willing and able to work with this class of response. If responses that are manifested as verbal reports can be observed directly or indirectly, behaviorists will endeavor to address the issue of feelings. The important thing is that whatever the label is—"nervous," "blue," "sadistic impulse," "fusion of ego boundaries,"—the behaviorist attempts to specify concretely and precisely what responses occur when the label is used.

Behavioral specification sometimes clarifies that what is embraced by vague general labels may turn out to refer to familiar well-studied behavioral phenomena. For example, "motivation" may reduce to a particular deprivation state combined with a particular schedule of reinforcement. Similarly, what is involved when particular feelings or "emotions" are reported can be objectified by the measurement of certain autonomic responses and concomitant verbal self-report responses. For example, the reported pain in tension headache can be correlated with electromyographic fluctuations (124). Other reported feelings, like some "impulses," are detectable as minute overt responses also through the use of an electromyogram. Other kinds of measuring instruments may be necessary for other feelings.

Most behavior therapists do make use of reports of private events in therapy, especially if such events can be specified clearly. Furthermore, commonly used behavior therapy techniques are based on assumptions about the existence of private events for which no elaborate specification is undertaken. For example, systematic desensitization relies on asking the patient to evoke imaginal scenes depicting particular, anxiety-eliciting stimuli.

Some clinicians believe that behavior therapists deny that private events have any causal role in human behavior. This also is not accurate, at least not for most behavior therapists. Private events may control overt responses or other private (mental) events, and have been demonstrated to do so (125); there are, however, differences of opinion among behaviorists concerning the importance of private events in the explanation of behavior. For example, Pavlov and Hull were interested in private events as potentially measurable activities of the brain, worthy of research. Skinner, while agreeing with this view, made a sharp distinction between potentially measurable physiological activities and hypothetical private events. He regards the latter as mere explanatory fictions.

The Concern that Behavior Therapists Ignore or Deny the Importance of Relationship

PERHAPS in part because of the emphasis on specific empirical techniques in behavior therapy, there is a widespread belief that a behavioral approach necessarily denies the importance of the effect of person and relationship in therapy. Not so. In fact, the precise specification of personal and nonpersonal components of therapeutic techniques offers the best avenue toward the further elucidation of the complex effects of human relationships in the therapeutic process.

Social relationships are among the most important, albeit complex, biological and behavioral phenomena. Some behaviorist have even stated that the most important stimulus is the person. The research by Harlow and his colleagues has clearly demonstrated the profound influence of neonatal social rearing conditions on an individual's subsequent development (126). In addition, recent research with Pavlovian techniques has contributed evidence for the fact that large-scale behavioral responses having measurable physiological components, regularly and consistently occur during various types of social interaction (127, 128, 129, 130, 131, 132, 133, 134). Of even greater interest from a psychotherapeutic point of view is the observation that both the behavioral and autonomic indices of the usual reactions to conditioned fear and pain (produced by pairing a tone with an electric shock) can be abolished by social stimulation during these aversive conditions (129, 130, 131). In fact, this is the model of systematic desensitization: relaxed social interaction during situations previously conditioned to be aversive.

Several studies agree that for schizophrenic patients, normally reinforcing social stimuli appear to function as punishment (135, 136, 137, 138).

The effect of person and relationship cannot be ignored in behavior therapy or any therapy. Rather it must be recognized as a pervasive and profoundly important phenomenon. In dynamic psychotherapy, much effort goes into trying to understand what, early on in his development, the patient learned and from which persons. It is good dynamic therapy, good behavior therapy, and good sense to be alert to the often contrasting effects of particular persons on a patient's current life and treatment.

Behavior therapists are concerned with relationship, but generally are more concerned with explicit details of how the therapist can use social reinforcement, to alter particular behavior patterns therapeutically.

THE
EFFICACY
OF
BEHAVIOR
THERAPY

In this section, we shall discuss the efficacy of behavior therapy, and provide an overview of those problems for which the methods of behavior therapy have been particularly successful—and unsuccessful. First, however, we shall consider the overall appropriateness of a behavioral approach to psychiatric problems.

Etiology vs. Efficacy

Science of Causes *power to produce the desired result*

A common misconception about therapy is that the therapy for a particular problem must direct itself to the root cause of that problem. In this view, disorders of biological origin should be treated with biologically based therapies, while those with psychological origins should be treated psychotherapeutically.

In fact, there is no necessary relationship between the etiology of a problem and the nature of the treatment that is effective in ameliorating it. A disorder with an organic or neurophysiological etiology may be responsive to a biological therapy, but it may also be markedly improved by behavior therapy. Similarly, difficulties that have an environmental origin may be responsive to biological intervention, such as psychopharmologic treatment, as well as to a behavioral treatment.

Behavior therapy is based on learning principles and thus is particularly appropriate for treating the learned component of problems, whatever the etiology. Consider, for example, treatment for schizophrenia. Everyone is aware that drug treatments have been useful in the treatment of schizophrenics, but in addition many studies have shown that schizophrenics' behavior can become strikingly improved if the patients participate in a behavior therapy program (28). Another example is *Gilles de la Tourette's* syndrome. While it is true that this pattern of disordered behavior may have an organic basis, it has been established that it can be treated either pharmacologically or behaviorally. The antipsychotic drug, haloperidol, at times is an effective drug in providing symptom relief, but behavior therapy techniques have also been shown to be effective in reducing the characteristic multiple tics (139, 140). Another example is alcoholism, which seems to have sociological, psychological and biological determinants. Several behavior therapy methods seem to be at least moderately successful in eliminating alcoholics' drinking (141), or in enabling them to keep their drinking at a moderate level (87).

Research on the Efficacy of Behavior Therapy

THE *raison d'être* of any clinical intervention is improvement in the quality of the patient's life, in the form of relief from neurotic suffering, improved personal and family relationships and increased productivity and pleasure. The ultimate justification of a behavioral approach is the demonstration that behavioral procedures do indeed bring about such changes. In particular, it is important to ascertain whether behavioral procedures bring about such changes more often, to a greater degree, more quickly or at less cost—with clearly defined clinical problems—than do alternative psychotherapeutic procedures. Many of the published clinical reports describing the success of behavioral procedures for the treatment of particular disorders are persuasive. For example, patients with chronic, disabling problems who have failed to respond to other forms of psychotherapy have shown well-documented and substantial improvement with behavioral procedures. However, such clinical studies alone are not sufficient, for it is easy to be misled by the reporters' enthusiasm, or by genuine results mediated

[66]

by suggestion. Only carefully designed, controlled clinical inquiries can provide strong data for or against the efficacy of behavior therapy procedures.

The role of suggestion

Beginning at least as early as 1902 with the "suggestive therapeutics" of Forel (142), it has been widely appreciated that suggestion must be taken very seriously as one mechanism underlying improvement in any psychotherapy. The much later, startling demonstrations by Wolf (143) that suggestion plus ipecac (normally an emetic drug) can inhibit the nausea and vomiting of hyperemesis gravidarum, and by Rosenthal (144), that experimenter expectation can drastically influence even precisely measured things like the comparative learning ability of rats, has merely underscored the importance of this factor.

While suggestion as a mechanism for improvement with behavioral techniques can never be totally excluded, we must remember that the same is true for all psychotherapy and psychoanalysis. Moreover, for behavior therapy, there are many valuable studies using the multiple baseline type of design (see p. 73–74) where some of the patients' behaviors are treated while others are not. In a general way, one would expect the effects of suggestion to act on all the problem behaviors, whereas differential improvement in treated vs. untreated problem behaviors would seem to reflect the action of the specific procedures. (This is not an airtight argument, of course, because while these studies may eliminate patient expectation, they do not rule out therapist expectation.) In practice, however, most behavior therapists, like psychotherapists, expect, welcome and use some component of suggestion in their work.

Outcome measures

The emphasis in behavior therapy is on the patient's behavior, the specific focus of the intervention being on modification of the interaction between the patient and the environment. In line with this conceptual framework, treatment outcome is measured in terms of changes in the interaction between the patient and the environment, such as improvement in a desired behavior or decrease in maladaptive behavior. Ideally, the patient's behavior would be observed frequently in his natural environment either by the therapist or by other persons who would report to the therapist. This is not always feasible, however, and in such cases the therapist may use behavioral tests in his office or, if these are not possible, self-report measures which are sometimes quantified in the form of rating scales.

[68]

Some general comments

When behavior therapy is done properly evaluation is included as a part of the therapy. Although evaluation of outcome is much more common in behavior therapy than in other kinds of psychotherapy, the situation needs improvement in several respects. First, some behavior therapy methods have been inadequately evaluated. Second, extended follow-ups of patients have rarely been reported. Follow-up reports are generally short term, ranging from a few months to a year. This is an important matter; the goal of behavior therapy is to teach the patient adaptive behavior that will be maintained by the natural rewards occurring in his every-day environment. Third, many reports of behavior therapy do not give broad clinical data about the individual characteristics of patients treated or about the relevant particulars of their individual backgrounds.

In evaluating a behavior-therapeutic intervention, the clinical researcher can compare it with some kind of no-treatment control plan or with an alternative therapeutic approach. There are a number of variants of these two basic evaluative strategies. Two evaluation designs commonly used by behavior therapy researchers will be described here. First, the various treatments being evaluated can be compared within an individual case. This sort of individual subject design will be illustrated by studies of the use of reinforcement procedures to shape and maintain self-help and social behavior in chronic psychotic patients. Second, behavior therapy can be compared with other treatments by means of a comparison between an experimental group and control group in which patients are randomly assigned to the treatment groups. This type of design will be illustrated by a study evaluating systematic desensitization therapy.

Individual subject design

This research strategy is in the tradition of the physiological research of Claude Bernard and Pavlov. It is an especially powerful design for identifying the variables in the total treatment package that are crucial for modifying specific maladaptive behavior. With this procedure, each patient in the study is an experiment himself because he is exposed to each type of treatment or control procedure.

In one sort of individual subject evaluation, the behavior of the person receiving the treatment is measured repeatedly—prior to the intervention, during the time that the intervention is in effect, during a subsequent period of time while the intervention is briefly terminated and then again under the influence of the therapeutic intervention. The rationale behind this design is that if the patient's behavior improves during the periods when the therapy is being administered and is worse during the intitial period and any other time that he is not receiving therapy, the therapeutic intervention is presumed to be responsible for the change. In effect, the patient is his own no-treatment control. In another version of this design, some form of pseudo-therapy is used as the standard of comparison, rather than no treatment at all.

This type of evaluative strategy is well illustrated in a series of pioneering studies by Ayllon and Azrin (28). In their experiments, the behavior of a psychotic patient is first measured by a reliable method. The behavior might be dressing appropriately in the morning, getting to the dining room on time or working on an off-ward job. After the researchers have determined the extent to which the patient engages in the desired behavior, some sort of reinforcement, such as cigarettes, praise, or access to a valued activity is offered immediately following small improvements in behavior. This is called contingent reinforcement. Once the behavior has been appropriately modified, the reinforcers are either temporarily stopped or else made non-contingent, i.e., given whether or not the desired behavior is exhibited. Typically, the new pro-social behavior will deteriorate at this point—a fact suggesting that the temporal relationship between behavior and reinforcement is crucial for its maintenance. The final confirmation of efficacy is to reinstate the lapsed behavior by reinstating the contingency between the behavior and the reinforcer.

Another example of this procedure is given in a study (145) in which the goal was to have socially withdrawn psychotic patients give a normal social greeting to all persons they met. This is one step in teaching the behavioral components of socialization. Throughout the study, the patients were repeatedly greeted by various persons, and each patient's reactions were noted. Initially, the patients responded to none of the greetings. In a series of gradually changing therapeutic conditions, the patients were first given cigarettes every time they greeted a therapist and then gradually the reinforcers were extended to interactions with additional persons. As the experiment progressed, the cigarettes were given less and less consistently, with the result that the behavior came more and more to be supported by its natural social consequences. By the end of the training, each of the three patients was observed to greet all those he met, even strangers, although cigarettes were no longer offered. This type of research design is like the Claude Bernard model in which the same procedures are used with several patients. In this case, the three patients given this sequence of experimental treatments responded similarly; that is, the experiment was replicated three times.

Because of the controls used with each of the subjects, the researchers were able to show that it was the association between the greetings and the cigarettes that caused the improvement in each of the patients, rather than the passage of time, the attention received from the persons who greeted the patients, the personality of any of the therapists involved or the experience of meeting new people.

Using individual subject evaluation designs, many researchers (29, 146, 147) have shown that improvements in a great variety of self-help and pro-social behaviors can be generated and maintained by reinforcement therapy in psychotic, neurotic and mentally retarded patients.

Multiple-baseline design

Another individual subject evaluation design which is coming to be used more frequently for evaluating the effectiveness of a therapeutic program is the multiple-baseline design (148). In this strategy, several of the patient's problem behaviors are measured initially, instead of just one. The therapeutic intervention is then introduced for one of the behaviors, at the same time as all the behaviors are measured. If the intervention produces improvement in the target behavior but not in the others, it can be argued that there is something about the specific relation between the target behavior and the environmental modification that has produced the improvement —presumably because the other behaviors would have been equally subject to non-specific effects such as the passage of time, other aspects of the patient's life and the relationship with the therapist. The treatment procedure is then applied successively to each of the behaviors being measured; evaluation of the intervention is inherent in each such application. A multiple-baseline design was recently applied in the sequential removal of four discrete phobias by systematic desensitization therapy (149).

Experimental group/ control group design

This research strategy has proved useful in establishing the efficacy of psychopharmacological agents. In this sort of comparative evaluation, one group of patients receives some sort of behavior therapy, while another group receives one of the traditional forms of treatment. This design is addressed to the important questions of relative therapeutic efficacy and cost-effectiveness. By comparing the results obtained with standard procedures and with behavior therapy, researchers can begin to draw conclusions about whether the costs of introducing new procedures—including staff training, changes in supervision and record-keeping and so on—will be balanced by significant improvement in patient functioning.

This type of design is well illustrated in a study evaluating the treatment of phobic disorders with systematic desensitization (150). A description of systematic desensitization has already been given on pp. 17–22. Here we will be concerned only with research on its efficacy.

In a study by Paul (150), which is perhaps the best controlled clinical trial of desensitization therapy, subjects were college students who reported severe anxiety in public speaking situations. Each was concerned about his problem because of an institutional requirement that all undergraduates take a public speaking course. Each subject was randomly assigned to one of four groups after a detailed assessment that included objective evaluations of performance in a public speaking situation. One group received systematic desensitization therapy, a second received insight-oriented psychotherapy, the third received the same number of sessions of an "attention-placebo" procedure to control for nonspecific therapeutic aspects of the treatment situation and the fourth group received no treatment and therefore constituted a waiting list control. Finally, another control group was formed whose members were not contacted individually for assessment of their public speaking anxiety. These subjects had reported intense anxiety in public speaking situations, however, and could be compared with the waiting list controls for the possible effects of the preliminary assessment procedures. In the placebo therapy sessions, the subjects met with an interested therapist, but care was taken to avoid discussion of personal problems and any other interaction that might contain active ingredients of the treatments being evaluated. The five therapists used in the study had extensive experience in insight-oriented psychotherapy, and were given detailed training in the systematic desensitization and attention-placebo procedures. Each therapist treated three subjects in each of the three treatment groups; subjects were randomly assigned to therapists.

On the basis of self-report, physiological and behavioral criteria, the subjects treated by systematic desensitization were found to experience the greatest reduction in public speaking anxiety in a realistic test situation. The insight-oriented psychotherapy subjects and those treated by the attention-placebo procedure were next best, and both these groups did better than the waiting list and no-contact controls. The latter two did about the same. The greater efficacy of the desensitization procedure was still apparent in a two-year follow-up assessment, and there was no evidence of symptom substitution (151).

Many other investigators have conducted similar controlled clinical trials with subjects bothered by small-animal phobias and examination anxiety (62). These studies generally attest to the efficacy of systematic desensitization. One significant factor to be remembered in integrating these analogue studies, however, is that the subjects had volunteered for an experiment, rather than having sought professional help for a disabling problem (64). Nevertheless, this research contributes data affirming the power of systematic desensitization for the removal of maladaptive anxiety.

In another clinical evaluation of systematic desensitization (152), outpatients with classical phobias were treated by systematic desensitization, individual psychotherapy or group psychotherapy. The groups were well matched on clinical and other variables; treatment was conducted once weekly for about a year. Phobic symptoms improved most rapidly with desensitization. At the end of treatment and at follow-up one year later, more of the patients treated by desensitization were improved than by either of the other procedures. Although the ratings of social adjustment were less sensitive and reliable than the ratings of phobic symptoms, patients treated by desensitization also showed more improvement in work and leisure adjustment. The assessment procedures were designed to reveal any evidence of symptom substitution, but none was found. Later, the patients who had failed to respond adequately to the group psychotherapy procedure were treated with desensitization (153). Phobias in these patients improved a great deal more in four months of desensitization than they had in the previous two years.

Conclusions

We have given just a few examples from a growing body of evaluative research on the procedures of behavior therapy. To summarize the literature as a whole, we conclude that individual subject designs have demonstrated that therapies based on reinforcement principles do produce more improvements than no treatment at all; these improvements cannot be explained merely in terms of the effects of having a relationship with the therapist. Review of the numerous studies of desensitization suggests that this procedure produces measurable benefits for patients across a wide range of problems (62).

Much less is known about the efficacy of behavior therapy in comparison with other standard treatments. The evaluative research available suggests, however, that systematic desensitization is a more effective and efficient way to treat most phobias than re-educative interpretive psychotherapy, and that token economies and milieu therapy are about equally effective for hospitalized patients.

Many studies using the experiment group/control group comparison design have been undertaken only recently, and much additional information on the efficacy and cost-effectiveness of behavior therapy should be available within the next few years.

Efficacy of Behavior Therapy for Different Problems

BEHAVIOR therapy has been highly effective with phobic reactions, anxiety reactions (62), enuresis (115), stuttering (154), and tics associated with *Gilles de la Tourette's* syndrome (139, 140). For example, from a review of eighty-five reports of the application of systematic desensitization to nearly a thousand different patients, it was concluded that desensitization could be counted on to produce measurable benefits across a range of distressing problems in which anxiety was a primary concern (62).

Problems that have shown some improvement when treated by behavior therapy procedures include obsessive-compulsive behavior, hysteria, encopresis, psychological impotence, homosexuality, fetishes, frigidity, transvestism, exhibitionism, gambling, obesity, anorexia, insomnia and nightmares. Also quite responsive to reinforcement therapy are the relatively normal behavioral problems of children such as temper tantrums, head bumping, thumb sucking, refusal to eat and excessive scratching. Promising demonstrations and individual studies have been undertaken with respect to such problems in the home as excessive verbal

[79]

demands, rebellious behavior and sibling rivalry and, outside of the home, isolate behavior, elective mutism, hyperactivity and difficulties in social interaction with peers.

Token reinforcement systems have been shown to be effective in modifying classroom behavior problems such as classroom disruption, failure to study and low academic achievement (73). Chronic mental patients have learned a wide variety of appropriate social behaviors after the introduction of a token economy (71). Studies have shown that careful implementation of behavioral techniques can produce improvements in the verbal and non-verbal behavior of psychotic and schizophrenic children (155).

Behavioral treatments have been somewhat less successful with alcoholism and smoking, but procedures recently developed seem superior to those used in the past, and future clinical evaluations may be more successful. Finally, behavioral treatment of tics, other than those associated with *Gilles de la Tourette's* syndrome, has been somewhat disappointing, although there have been occasional successes.

Behavior therapy procedures require that the problem behavior can be clearly specified. That is, the therapist needs to be able to develop an objective definition of the response that is to be removed or taught to the patient. Thus certain kinds of problems treated by dynamic psychotherapy are simply not appropriate candidates for behavior therapy. In particular, the patient who comes because of an existential crisis—"Who am I? Where am I going?"—is not an appropriate candidate for behavior therapy. This quasi-philosophical problem does not lend itself to an approach that deals with specific identifiable behavior in particular environmental contexts. It is possible, however, that a patient who describes his problem in this way actually has some specific behavioral deficits that may underlie his existential difficulties or occur alongside them. A careful behavioral analysis of the patient's difficulties should reveal whether this is the case.

RELATIONSHIP TO DYNAMIC PSYCHIATRY

There is general agreement that psychiatry has benefited and will benefit further from incorporating concepts and techniques derived from the behavioral tradition. Among behaviorists —including even some of the members of this Task Force—there is much less agreement that behavior therapists have a great deal to learn from dynamic psychiatrists.

Some of us on this Task Force, however, especially those with training and experience in both the dynamic and the behavioral tradition, feel strongly that there is much value in the accumulated clinical experience and skills of psychiatrists whose training and work has been in the clinical, dynamic tradition. There are many

genuine points of contact between dynamic psychotherapy and behavior therapy that we hope will con-
tinue to be explored productively by psychotherapists and behavior therapists. We hope especially that
the number of people with solid backgrounds and interests in both traditions will increase. We see this as the
best avenue toward meaningful integration and cross-
fertilization of the two approaches. In a later section of
this report, we will present some educational proposals
to facilitate reaching that goal, while in this section we
will discuss some areas within psychiatry where there is
an overlapping of interest and experience.

Psychotherapy:
Inherent Processes of
Operant Conditioning

IN 1955, Greenspoon (156) published an important
paper on verbal conditioning in which he suggested
that the patient's verbal behavior in therapy was con-

trolled by reinforcement from the therapist in the form of his nodding or saying "mmm-hmm." Ever since, there has been a growing awareness that reinforcement operates in all psychotherapy. Jerome Frank (157) expanded people's awareness of the behavioral conditioning implicit in all psychotherapies when he called attention to the techniques and results of brain-washing, primitive and modern. His review supported the idea that people tend to change their attitudes to conform to what they have been conditioned repeatedly to say. In this way, verbal conditioning can be a mediator for attitude change and possibly for correlated behavior change as well. Another aspect of psychotherapy that can be looked at from a learning point of view is that in traditional therapy unpleasant autonomic responses are elicited in the patient and then not punished (158). Franz Alexander, for example, spoke of the "corrective emotional experience" that the patient has with a therapist who, unlike significant others in the patient's past, does not punish sexual and aggressive feelings. These two examples suggest that reinforcement principles studied by experimental psychologists specializing in operant conditioning are of very great importance in all psychotherapy.

Group Therapy and
Family Therapy:
In Vivo *Behavioral Shaping*

GROUP therapy, with its *in vivo* display of habitual maladaptive social behaviors, is an ideal medium in which to use therapist-mediated social reinforcement as an agent for behavioral change (103, 118). In group therapy and family therapy (100, 159), the therapist has the enormous practical advantage of seeing maladaptive behavioral patterns unfold and develop *in vivo*. As a result, he can shift his strategy from relatively weak techniques of attitude change through verbal conditioning, and of "corrective" extinction of emotional experiences, to a much more rapid and powerful method, and one which is especially appropriate for patients whose primary problems center around their relationships with others. Many patients have problems that involve habitual, subtle, maladaptive interpersonal behaviors. Bringing them into a group or family setting where they actually experience problems with other people can be extraordinarily important and catalytic both diagnostically in terms of what patients' actual maladaptive behaviors are and therapeutically, because

[86]

these settings allow for the direct behavioral shaping of alternative modes of behavior.

Some therapists will prefer to emphazie the objective behavioral procedures used in such settings, stressing the use of contingent social reinforcement for increasingly appropriate behavior and other related behavioral intervention methods. Others will prefer to conceptualize the therapy in dual terms, feeling that training and experience in both dynamic psychiatry and behavior therapy are useful here. In this view, the therapist can be more effective if he can understand and work with the phenomena of unconscious motivation, and if he also is skilled in behavioral techniques.

Sex Therapy:
The Interface with
Couples Therapy

THE treatment of sexual problems is an area where behavior therapy has performed well and it seems to hold much promise for further development. Examples include work with impotent men (160), fridgid women (161) and homosexual men (162, 163). The well known work of Masters and Johnson (164) is basically a behavioral approach, although its inventors derived their treatment method from common sense and their detailed knowledge of sexual physiology, rather than from learning principles or an experimental evaluation. The end goal of healthy sexual adjustment involves an adaptation to the needs and feelings of another person, which suggests that couples therapists of long experience with married and unmarried couples and behavior therapists working with sexual problems may have a great deal to learn from each other.

Toward a More
Scientific Psychiatry

ANOTHER area where psychoanalytically trained clinicians and behavior therapists may have something to learn from each other is in the general attempt to make the practice of psychiatry more scientific. The behaviorists, looking precisely with well developed scientific methods at defined segments of behavior that are part of clinical practice, can add much rigor to the dynamic therapists' understanding of what patients are complaining about and the mechanisms of improvement or behavior change. On the other hand, some analysts may already be actively and effectively interested in important, unlearned determinants of human behavior, such as genetics and biochemistry, and in non-experimental but basic disciplines like anthropology and ethology. Their knowledge of these fields could contribute much to the behavior therapist's approach inasmuch as behaviorists tend to concentrate only on learned behavior and often neglect the cultural context of the behavior.

De Facto *Integration*

CONSIDERABLE *de facto* integration of behavioral and psychoanalytic ideas already exists. In their insistence on conflictual areas being faced and "worked through" in a progressive way, psychodynamic therapists, including Freud, typically approach the phobic patient in a manner reminiscent of the approach of systematic desensitization. Recent reports (109) suggest that *in vivo* desensitization is almost always considerably superior to imaginal desensitization, again underscoring the need for patients to "work through" their phobic behavior in the real life situation. Various techniques and gimmicks have been used by both behavior therapists and psychoanalytic therapists to encourage patients to make a gradual approach to the phobic situation.

While we have mentioned a few examples of compatibility and partial integration between behavior therapy and dynamic psychiatry, these are not meant to deny or smooth over very real and substantial differences in emphasis, concept and procedure. Rather, we hope to underscore the feeling of some members of the Task Force that the analyst and behaviorist have much to say to each other.

PREVENTION

It is unlikely that the ranks of mental health professionals will ever be sufficient to meet the challenge of the increasing numbers of emotionally disturbed persons. Many professionals have come to feel that the only practical solution to this growing problem is to focus on the prevention of emotional disturbance and behavior disorders, and on the training of paraprofessionals. The techniques of behavior therapy have been applied successfully in a variety of preventive mental health settings and can be readily used by paraprofessionals as well, so behavior therapy is particularly suited to a preventive approach to mental health (165).

Prevention

The prevention of emotional disturbance can occur at several levels. First, prevention programs can help individuals acquire sufficient skill to cope with everyday living and to avoid developing mental health problems. Second, prevention programs can prepare individuals for periods of undue stress, especially during critical periods in their lives. Third, these programs can also train chronically handicapped persons, including former patients, in the skills necessary to remain and function in the community. Behavior therapy methods can be effective at each of these levels of prevention. Preventive mental health approaches have tended to center on the normal life crises, especially the critical developmental points. These approaches can be directed toward parents, teachers and others involved in child care and family service.

Parent effectiveness training or training for parenthood can make use of learning principles and behavior therapy in a number of ways. Training manuals in child management (166, 167, 168) provide efficient and effective guides for parents in the day-to-day management of their developing child. These manuals describe basic principles of learning and behavior analysis as applied to child management, give examples of a variety of "problems" in parent-child interaction and suggest non-punitive approaches to child management that are easily adapted to other family situations. Parent effectiveness seminars, discussion groups and courses offer further preventive mental health opportunities. These seminars, often led by both pediatricians and child mental health professionals, may be conducted in community settings for expectant as well as new parents. Such seminars deal with normal and abnormal aspects of the child's physical, emotional and cognitive development, focus on childhood and parental developmental tasks, and teach those responsible for children to use behavioral principles in deriving guidelines for the management of these tasks, as well as for the avoidance or management of potential problems at various stages of development. Finally, these discussion groups provide a setting for ongoing consultation with parents in regard to their questions and concerns about their own and their children's development.

Another major preventive mental health approach focuses on the professionals who provide child care and family service. These include teachers, counselors, social workers, child care workers, and probation officers. Child and family development are essential topics in the training of these professionals. In addition, training manuals that explain learning principles and provide behavioral guidelines for child management (169, 170) have proved helpful. Ongoing behavioral consultation with teachers and others involved in child care has provided the opportunity to prevent or reduce problems in child management in their natural settings. Behavioral consultation with pre-school teachers (32) and elementary and high school teachers (171) has reduced or eliminated problem behaviors such as age-inappropriate crawling, crying, isolation, hyperactivity, disruptions and inattention. Programs with delinquent youths have also utilized this type of consultation (172) with some success. With appropriate training and ongoing consultation for parents and child care professionals, preventive mental health programs may be developed for wide segments of our population.

Agents of therapeutic change

The possibility of training persons who do not have backgrounds in psychology or psychiatry also holds great promise for dealing with emotional disturbances at preventive levels. The training of community counselors in behavior modification methods and the training of high school and college students and others in behavioral techniques provide the opportunity for increased manpower to prevent or reduce the extent of emotional disturbance. In their preventive mental health activities, trained paraprofessionals would be involved with their peers—other students, community residents and so on, i.e., persons with whom they have common bonds. They would provide ongoing consultation with families, community associations, student groups and others in this work. Among the sorts of persons who have been used as therapists in behavioral treatment programs are psychiatric nurses (173), teachers and pupils (174), parents (175), other adults (176), high school students and ghetto residents (177).

The literature suggests that such persons, with a minimum of training and guidance, can be highly effective in carrying out behavior therapy programs. Regular supervision and consultation with mental health professionals trained in behavior therapy are extremely important, of course, and must be an integral part of any paraprofessional mental health program.

ABUSES
AND
CONCERNS

Behavior therapy shares will all other therapies the possibility of being used improperly. In this section, we discuss some abuses of behavior therapy and suggest some ways that these abuses could be avoided.

Inadequate Training
in Basic Science

CALLING a treatment program "behavioral," or labeling a care management system "a token economy" does not make it so if basic behavioral science fundamentals have been neglected. This is especially a hazard in a field like behavior therapy because to the person with little or no training it all seems so deceptively simple: "It's just a matter of reward and punishment, right?" Some published reports describe abysmally designed treatment programs; many worse examples never appear in the archival literature.

Partially trained and partially educated individuals are specialists in techniques only. Too often their inadequate training results in their using only a single treatment technique and thus misusing it (98). Persons with limited training should be supervised by comprehensively trained therapists who decide on the kind of treatment, the duration of treatment and when it should be applied, only after considering the possible consequences for the patient, his family and his associates.

Insufficient Supervised Clinical Experience

MANY of the clinical vignettes cited as criticism of behavior therapy seem to have resulted from the therapist's having had an inadequate amount of supervised clinical experience. Once a newly trained behavior therapist has learned a given behavioral method, he might be tempted to apply that procedure to all cases he encounters, perhaps because the methods seem to be easy to learn and to apply. As in the previous example, this may lead to overuse and hence abuse of a single treatment technique.

Many behavior therapists feel that extensive clinical supervision is necessary to ensure not only that the novice acquires an array of behavior therapy methods, but also that he gains an appreciation of other factors that are important for therapeutic activity. These factors—support, guidance, advice, encouragement, reassurance, and clarification—while difficult to define and hard to conceptualize in ways productive of objective data, are still important aspects of the therapeutic process.

[99]

The Latent Function
of Social Control

BEHAVIOR therapy approaches have been misused in some instances when the focus was on changing the individual, instead of the oppressive sociopolitical or environmental realities (178). This has generally occurred in correctional institutions, schools and mental hospitals, but can occur in any situation. Therapists must be on guard against requests for treatment that take the form "make him 'behave,'" in which the intention of the request is to make the person conform. This risk does seem greater with behavior therapy than with psychotherapeutic approaches, because it is possible to objectify behavior therapy to such an extent that some behavioral technicians can lose sight of the importance of responding empathically to another human being and respecting his rights. One safeguard against this is to obtain the patient's informed agreement about the goals and methods of the therapy program whenever possible.

The Ethical Problem
of Coercive Manipulation

DESPITE the extensive discussions of ethical issues by public and professional groups, there does not seem to be a real ethical problem for skillful clinicians who practice behavior therapy. Therapy without manipulation is a mirage that disappears on close scrutiny (118). The competent therapist is usually aware of his capacity to influence the patient and works together with him to achieve the goal of a better level of functioning.

The Non-Therapeutic Use of Punishment: Rationalizing Sadistic Behavior

BEHAVIORAL regimens may be used to punish patients vindictively, with the excuse that the punishment is part of a planned therapeutic program. This rationalization of possibly sadistic behavior may be a particular hazard with patient groups that arouse intense feelings of anger, disgust or scorn in some therapists—e.g., groups like heroin addicts, deteriorated alcoholics; and certain sexually deviant patients.

This serious abuse can be controlled in several ways: first, aversive methods should be carried out under the surveillance of the therapists's clinical peers and colleagues; second, aversive methods especially should be used only with the patient's informed consent; third, the therapist should abandon any method, especially any aversive method, for which objective data fail to show that it significantly helps patients; fourth, the behavioral therapist should understand himself and his covert emotional needs. If the therapist is aware of precisely what reinforces his own behavior, he can avoid exploitation in his work with patients.

[102]

Concerns About
Specific Techniques

IN this section, we mention as examples a few techniques that one frequently hears criticized in discussions about behavior therapy. Some of the concerns expressed are equally applicable to other behavioral techniques.

Covert sensitization

The purpose of this procedure is to build up an avoidance response to the stimulus associated with a problem behavior like excessive drinking, over-eating or homosexuality. The patient first imagines the stimulus, and then follows it in his imagination with the thought of an unpleasant event. Patients are reported to manifest no urge or temptation for the formerly desirable stimulus after this sort of therapy. The critical problem with this procedure is that while it appears to have some basis in principles of learning, few if any studies have been published so far that have critically evaluated the method (179). Despite the lack of scien-

[103]

tific evaluation, it seems that this technique, apparently because of its simplicity, is becoming widely used. Scientifically, however, the technique is on shaky ground because nothing in it is subject to direct observation and measurement.

Flooding

In flooding, the patient is exposed to vivid representations of the stimuli that elicit his fear, or to the actual stimuli, in circumstances in which he cannot avoid the stimuli. This technique has a potential for harm, because if the patient quits the therapy, his escape from the threatening situation serves to increase his anxiety level when he encounters the stimuli again. This pitfall can generally be avoided through the therapist's providing social support in the form of the presence of other unfeared persons, by asking the patient to engage actively in competing behavior, or by explaining this hazard ahead of time to the patient, so as to obtain his advance permission for the therapy situation to be structured so that he will not be able to leave the flooding stimuli prematurely and with self-destructive effects. Some clinical studies have supported the value of flooding techniques (109), but this procedure has so far been studied with much less thoroughness than systematic desensitization.

[104]

Implosive therapy

The only difference between flooding and implosive therapy is that in the latter, the stimuli are chosen for presentation in therapy on the basis of psychoanalytic theory; cues are used from those dynamic areas thought to be the basic problem of the patient (180). Thus, this method of therapy is a combination of psychoanalytic theory and procedures derived from experimental psychology research. One concern is that the method appears to accept the traumatic event as being of primary importance, despite evidence that a single traumatic event is seldom found, except in the case of war or accident neuroses. Another concern, of course, is the absence of controlled clinical evaluations of this procedure. Most important, however, is the danger that this procedure, perhaps even more than flooding, may put certain patients at risk.

RESEARCH
NEEDS

The future of a new direction in a clinical discipline depends ultimately on research: laboratory research that provides the basis for new clinical procedures and clinical research that determine the efficacy and cost-effectiveness of new preventive and therapeutic programs.

Behavior therapy, a new approach in psychiatry, enjoys a special relationship to research for several reasons. First, behavior therapy developed largely from experimental psychology (see pp. 4–9). It is this basis in experimental behavioral science that chiefly distinguishes behavior therapy from alternative clinical approaches to the understanding and treatment of psychiatric disorders. Second, the methodology of behavior therapy requires the clinician to describe the psychotherapeutic enterprise in as explicit, objective and quantitative terms as possible. This applies to his identification of the patient's dysfunction, its relation to other observable events, the goals of treatment, the treatment procedures themselves, and finally, the assessment of the effects of the whole intervention. A clinical approach conducted by these rules of procedure lends itself especially well to controlled clinical studies. Third, the treatment of the individual patient often proceeds as a controlled clinical experiment with a single subject. Behavioral analysis consists in part in the manipulation of environmental and behavioral variables thought to be functionally related to the patient's difficulties (see pp. 13–16). If the patient fails to respond favorably, more clinical data are obtained, the behavioral analysis is continued and new or modified clinical hypotheses are tested in the behavioral treatment.

Research accomplishments, areas of current interest, and research needs are mentioned directly or indirectly in nearly every other section of this report. Here, we will simply indicate the scope of research in behavior therapy and describe some areas of special promise.

Laboratory research

Basic research in the behavioral laboratory adds to our knowledge of the environmental determinants of behavior and their relationship to intra-organismic events and, in turn, to our knowledge of the origin and course of some behavioral disturbances. Research in this category includes animal experimental paradigms of some human psychopathological states, such as animal models of phobic states (181), depression (182) and addiction to opiates (183).

Research on the experimental analysis of psychopathological states in human subjects uses the principles of learning and the methods of experimental psychology to find the environmental variables that maintain particular disordered behaviors. Some of the classical psychoneuroses have been subjected to this kind of analysis (184, 185, 186).

Behavioral engineering research

Another current research area is the development of instruments that would facilitate the learning of more adaptive behavioral problems. Devices have been developed to aid patients in gaining control over specific behavioral problems such as cigarette smoking (187), stuttering (110) and other speech disorders, and interpersonal difficulties such as faulty communication practices in troubled marriages (188). Some of the devices that have been developed can be worn inconspicuously by the person in natural settings. This approach to the modification of problem behaviors has several

[109]

obvious advantages, among them the potentiality for continuous application of the treatment, economical dissemination of behavior modification procedures and uniformity of consequences. Most important of all, perhaps, is that the use of portable instruments helps the patient develop self-control; that is, it is he who decides whether the apparatus is to be used.

Research on use of drugs

A much neglected but very promising research area involves the use of pharmacologic agents to increase the efficacy of behavioral procedures (189). Much is being learned about the way specific drugs affect specific behavioral processes. This suggests a beneficial marriage of behavioral pharmacology and behavior therapy. The potential of this area has already been demonstrated by a few applications—the use of intravenous barbiturates to facilitate systematic desensitization therapy (190), for example.

Biofeedback research

An exciting new area of research concerns the use of biofeedback techniques to alter physiological functions for therapeutic purposes. In this work, subjects are given informative feedback about the state of one of their physiological response systems, and are reinforced for changing the level of response of that system in the direction requested. Research in this area is only just beginning to be extended to clinical problems, but it has obvious important implications for psychosomatic medicine. Preliminary clinical studies show the promise of these techniques for the treatment of, among other things, early labile essential hypertension (191), Reynaud's disease (192), cardiac arrhythmias (193), and tension and migraine headaches (124, 194, 195).

Research on comparative efficacy

The research area of highest priority is the controlled clinical comparison of behavioral procedures with alternative (nonbehavioral) treatment methods for specific psychiatric disorders. As described elsewhere in this report, a few such studies have been conducted, such as those comparing systematic desensitization with more traditional psychiatric approaches for the treatment of phobia-like disorders. Analogous studies are needed across a wide range of behavioral interventions. Several such studies have been undertaken only very recently.

TRAINING
RECOMMENDATIONS

The incorporation of new and controversial materials into the curricula of medical schools and residency training programs inevitably lags behind their development on the research front. This is certainly the case with behavior therapy. We will first consider the present status of training in behavior therapy outside of psychiatry, then assess its status in psychiatric training programs and finally consider what recommendations might be made for teaching a behavioral approach in psychiatric settings.

Status of behavior therapy training in psychology

The behavioral approach is rapidly gaining interest and attention in the psychology departments of colleges and universities. A recent survey (196) found that

84% of a random sample of schools offering doctoral level training in psychology have courses in behavior modification. Post-doctoral training in behavior therapy is also available at several universities. Only 19% of undergraduate colleges offer a course in behavior modification, but it is likely that a high percentage of the colleges without a specific course in behavior therapy include some of this material in courses of general psychology or abnormal psychology. For the most part, the aim of undergraduate colleges is not professional training but liberal education.

Status of behavior therapy training in medical schools

Didactic material in behavior principles and training in behavior therapy is seemingly only arbitrarily incorporated into medical education at the pre-medical, medical school and residency levels. Since most medical schools have no requirement in these areas, medical students may or may not have had exposure to learning principles and behavior therapy in college courses in psychology and the social sciences. We believe that a course in pscyhology with special attention to the experimental analysis of behavior should be recommended in pre-medical curricula. Just as pre-medical basic science courses are requisite to an understanding of a patient's physical problems, knowledge of learning principles would add immeasurably to an understanding of emotional difficulties.

There is a critical problem in terms of the availability of medical school faculty with interest, knowledge and experience in behavioral science. Because it is still true that few psychiatrists have strong backgrounds in a behavioral approach, it often happens that medical students have more of a background in the experimental analysis of behavior than their clinical instructors in psychiatry.

Many medical students know that this is an important and developing area but find few courses in behavior therapy and learning principles in the medical school curriculum. A recent survey (197) showed that while 86% of American medical schools offer some material on these topics during the four-year curriculum, in many instances only a token amount is offered. Thus the median duration of required course material on behavior therapy is three hours. The median duration of elective course material, presumably taken by a small fraction of students, is twenty hours. In spite of this lack of behavioral training in medical school curricula, however, questions on behavior theory and technique often appear on state and national board examinations and on psychiatry board examinations.

TRAINING RECOMMENDATIONS

Status of behavior therapy training in psychiatry

The opportunity for psychiatric residents to learn behavioral procedures varies with the particular program, but is generally meager. A survey (197) of eighty randomly selected programs in the United States indicated that 11% offer no material of any kind in behavior therapy. For those who do offer some didactic material on a behavioral approach, the median duration of this exposure is only ten hours. Only a few programs (11%) have a required behavior therapy practicum, including demonstrations of behavioral procedures and clinical clerkships; these have a median duration of two months. We feel there should be more opportunity for training in behavior therapy than now exists.

Recommendations for training programs in psychiatric settings

The setting for the teaching of behavior therapy is an important consideration. Departments of psychology and psychiatry have an opportunity to combine their individual talents for the benefit of the trainee in behavior therapy. The experimental analysis of behavior has historically been the province of departments of psychology, while clinical treatment and availability of patients is usually associated with departments of psychiatry. We agree with Poser (198) that behavior therapy is best taught where there is an active behavior therapy service.

A training program in behavioral psychiatry should, therefore, combine access to a clinical setting—i.e., an active behavior therapy service, and access to a research laboratory whose emphasis is experimental studies of learning.

The kind of training is also important. Because the behavioral analysis or assessment is crucial for competent behavior therapy, training in behavior therapy at both the medical school and residency levels should emphasize basic principles of learning and their application to a behavioral analysis and the design of a treatment plan. Some training and supervised experience in the conduct of a variety of behavioral procedures is also desirable, especially at the residency level.

The specific course content and method of instruction for medical school and residency training in behavior therapy will necessarily reflect the interests, experience and perhaps prejudices of those responsible for the task. Descriptions of courses for first-year medical students (199) and for psychiatric residents (200), have recently become available, and do indeed reflect a variety of approaches.

As the efficacy of a behavioral approach has become

better established, the demand by practicing psychiatrists for instruction in the theory and practice of behavior therapy has grown. At present there are only a
few behavior therapy workshops and continuing education courses available (201).

One of the things now needed most in medical
education is a much broader, deeper and earlier emphasis on basic behavioral science fundamentals, and
many more well rounded experienced clinicians and
teachers who are able to use a behavioral approach and
behavioral techniques as a part of their practice.

BASIC
CONCEPTS
AND
PRINCIPLES

The basic vocabulary and conceptual framework of behavior therapy reflects the strong empirical and theoretical influence of experimental pychology. The principles and procedures of behavior therapy result from both conditioned reflex (Pavlovian) research and operant conditioning (Skinnerian) research on learning. The material in this technical section emphasizes operant concepts and principles because we believe the reader is likely to be less conversant with these than with Pavlovian concepts.

The Basic Elements:
Stimulus and Response

THE experimental psychologist views behavior as an interaction between the individual and his environment. The constituents of this interaction are conventionally formulated in terms of stimulus and response events. At the most fundamental level, stimuli are identified with environmental segments, and responses are defined by the activities of individuals. The technical referents of both terms, however, are far more complex than their ordinary meanings suggest.

First, the environment can be divided into several classes of stimuli based on the role of such events in behavioral interactions. One class, *eliciting stimuli*, regularly precedes and elicits reflexive or relatively fixed and stereotyped responses. A second class, *reinforcing stimuli* or *reinforcers*, consists of environmental events that follow responses and influence the frequency with which these responses will recur in future behavioral interactions. And the third major class of behaviorally important environmental events, the *discriminative stimuli*, generally precedes and accompanies responses. In contrast to eliciting stimuli, discriminative stimuli do not elicit responses in the reflexive sense. Rather, discriminative stimuli influence the frequency of those

[120]

responses that have previously been followed by reinforcers in their presence.

Second, individuals' activities can be separated into
two broad classes based principally on the temporal
ordering of the controlling stimulus and the response.
One class, reflexive responses or *respondents,* is controlled by the frequency of prior-occurring eliciting
stimuli and is basically determined by the "involuntary"
constitutional reflex endowment of the organism, e.g.,
salivation or startle. The other class, *instrumental* or
operant responses, consists of emitted activities, the frequency of which is controlled by the occurrence of
reinforcing stimuli that follow such "voluntary" responses.

Respondent Conditioning

SINCE at least the time of Pavlov, the same set of
stimulus and response concepts has provided a scientifically useful basis for describing and experimentally

analyzing increasingly more complex behavioral interactions. Early laboratory studies, for example, provided the first systematic respondent conditioning account of how environmental events (e.g., the sound of a bell), initially ineffective in changing response activities, can come to elicit respondents (e.g., salivation) when paired repeatedly with eliciting stimuli (e.g., food). If the sound of the bell (the *conditioned stimulus*) is subsequently presented a number of times without the food (the *unconditioned stimulus*), the magnitude and frequency of the salivation elicited by the conditioned stimulus *(CS)* diminish, and *respondent extinction* occurs. When a period of time intervenes between such extinction sessions and subsequent presentations of the conditioned stimulus, however, *spontaneous recovery* is observed in the form of an increase in the magnitude and frequency of the *conditioned response (CR)* elicited by the conditioned stimulus.

Furthermore, the power to elicit a respondent, which is developed in one CS by conditioning, extends to other stimuli *(generalization)*. There is a *gradient of generalization*, that is, the degree of generalization is determined by the similarities and differences between the other stimuli and the CS. Because the stimuli other than the CS differ with respect to the magnitude and frequency with which they elicit the CR, *discrimination* also occurs. Indeed, discrimination can be made increasingly more pronounced by repeated pairings of the unconditioned stimulus *(UCS)* only with the specific CS (i.e., respondent conditioning) while insuring that the occurrence of other stimuli is not paired with the UCS (i.e., respondent extinction).

These basic principles of respondent conditioning have been elaborated in numerous laboratory and clinical-experimental studies since Russian researchers first introduced this systematic approach to behavior analysis. It has been convincingly demonstrated, for example, that *second-* or *higher-order conditioning* can occur when a well-established CS is paired with a neutral stimulus. The neutral stimulus acquires the power to elicit the respondent CR. Although it has not been empirically determined just how far this process can be carried, the development of eliciting properties by CSs two or three steps removed from the original UCS is not uncommon. And the intensive investigative effort, principally Russian in origin, to extend the conceptual framework of respondent conditioning to encompass verbal stimuli and semantic responses would seem to be important for both the theory and practice of behavior therapy.

Operant Conditioning

ELICITED respondents of the type that have provided the primary focus for such basic and important Pavlovian or classical conditioning analyses characterize only a relatively small proportion of the behavioral interactions of higher organisms. The most prominent aspects of such advanced repertoires are represented by the instrumental or operant category for which there is no environmental eliciting stimulus and which is generally described as "voluntary" or emitted. The frequency of occurrence of an operant is chiefly determined by the environmental events that follow the emitted response. When these environmental consequences involve the appearance of stimuli that increase the probability that the response they followed will recur in the future, the term *appetitive* or *positive reinforcer* is applied. When, on the other hand, the disappearance or postponement of an environmental stimulus as a consequence of an operant response results in an increased probability that the response will recur in the future, an *aversive* or *negative reinforcer* is defined. That is, reinforcers are always defined by their effects on the subsequent frequency of the immediately preceding response: both positive and negative reinforcers increase the frequency of the preceding response.

[124]

The effects of reinforcement

Over the past three decades, a broad range of animal laboratory and human experimental studies has provided important insights into the principles that determine the acquisition, maintenance and modification of operant behavior. The basic observation is that the rate of emission of an operant response already in the organism's repertoire can be readily increased by following occurrences of the response with a reinforcing stimulus *(operant conditioning)*.

Beyond this, it has been possible to make explicit the process called *shaping*, whereby a combination of operant conditioning and extinction can change existing simple responses into new and more complex performances.

Important theoretically for the shaping process is the observation that a reinforcing stimulus not only strengthens the particular response that precedes it, but also results in an increase in the frequency of many other bits of behavior (i.e., raises the individual's general activity level). In shaping, reinforcers are initially presented following a response similar to or approximating the desired one. Since this tends to increase the strength of various other similar behaviors, a response still closer to that desired can be selected from this new array and followed by reinforcing stimuli. Continued narrowing and refinement of the response criteria required for reinforcement leads progressively to new arrays of available behavior. In this way, by successive and progressive approximation, a new and desired performance can be shaped. The importance of this simple but fundamental and powerful shaping process for the development and modification of behavior cannot be overstated, since the weight of available evidence suggests that a careful and systematic application of such procedures is sufficient to establish or alter any operant performance of which the organism is physically capable. It is of enormous clinical importance, since many patient behaviors can only effectively be changed through shaping. Without shaping, one might wait forever for a mute patient to talk with feeling about his problems in order to be able to reinforce such a response.

The fact that changes in behavior are not always brought about by deliberate and systematic manipulation of the environment, however, has led to an analysis of *superstitious behavior*. An environmental stimulus may, by chance, follow a response, resulting in the adventitious strengthening of that response. If this happens repeatedly, the individual may learn quite elaborate sequences of superstitious behavior which have absolutely nothing to do with the reinforcing stimuli that are influencing their occurrence (e.g., the exhortations of the gambler do not produce winning dice combinations; they persist because they are occasionally followed by "7" or "11").

The powerful effects of reinforcing stimulus consequences in establishing and maintaining operant behavior suggest that withholding or withdrawing of such reinforcers *(operant extinction)* will have comparably powerful effects on the strength of responses previously followed by reinforcing stimuli. Indeed, such extinction procedures do reduce the frequency of response, although the reduction is not usually immediate. Rather, after the onset of extinction, the initial effect is often a brief increase in the frequency as well as the force and variability of the response followed by reinforcement. The extent to which operant responding persists in the absence of reinforcing environmental stimulus consequences *(resistance to extinction)* depends, of course, on the interaction of many complex influences including motivational factors, e.g., level of deprivation. But both laboratory and clinical experimental evidence now confirms that the single most important variable affecting the course of operant extinction is the schedule of reinforcement on which the performance was previously maintained.

A *schedule of reinforcement* is a rule that specifies which occurrences of a particular operant response will be followed by a reinforcing stimulus. The basic observation from which these rules are derived is that a reinforcing environmental stimulus does not necessarily have to follow every occurrence of an operant response in order for the form or frequency of responding to be maintained or modified. In reality, intermittency in the occurrence of reinforcers following operant responses is the most common state of affairs, and laboratory experimental analysis of the almost limitless number of possible schedules of intermittent reinforcement has begun to shed some light on the many subtleties that characterize these important mainsprings of behavior control.

Stimulus control

The detailed experimental analysis of schedules of reinforcement has shown the importance of *stimulus control*. The occurrence of a reinforcing stimulus following an operant response not only increases the probability that the response will recur, but also contributes to bringing that response under control of the other environmental stimuli present when reinforcement occurred. After the response has been reinforced in a particular environmental setting a number of times, the response will tend to be more frequent in that setting than elsewhere. A *discriminative stimulus* is an environmental setting in the presence of which a particular operant response is highly probable because it has previously been reinforced there. It is important to recognize, however, that discriminative stimuli do not elicit responses as in the respondent or reflex paradigm, but rather they set the occasion on which a

[128]

behavior has previously been reinforced. This controlling power of a discriminative stimulus develops gradually, and at least several occurrences of a reinforcer following a response in the presence of a discriminative stimulus are required before the stimulus effectively controls the behavior.

Discriminative stimulus control is not an entirely selective process, however, since reinforcement of a response in the presence of one stimulus increases the tendency of that individual to respond not only in the presence of that stimulus but also in the presence of other stimuli with similar properties *(stimulus generalization)*. Furthermore, following an operant behavior with a reinforcer results not only in an increase in the frequency of that response but also in an increase in the frequency of similar responses *(response generalization)*. It is not always clear from simple observation which stimulus or which property of a stimulus is the controlling factor, or which aspects of an operant performance a stimulus in fact controls. Both laboratory research and clinical experience have documented the hazard of assuming that the similarity casually observed between stimuli or responses provided an adequate explanation of generalization. The best way to decide which of the many detailed aspects of a stimulus complex exercises critical control over certain responses is by means of experimentation.

The other major cornerstone of the stimulus control process is *discrimination*. A discrimination between two stimuli is said to obtain when an individual behaves differently in the presence of each. *Stimulus discrimination* is pronounced under conditions that provide *differential reinforcement;* this process is most clearly seen when there is a high probability that a reinforcer will follow a given response in the presence of one stimulus, and a low or zero probability that the reinforcing stimulus will follow the response in the presence of another stimulus. The extent of the generalization between two stimuli will, of course, influence the rapidity and stability with which a discrimination can be formed. The careful application of differential reinforcement procedures can bring about remarkably precise control by highly selective aspects of a stimulus complex. Instructions can enhance this process by telling the individual about features of the environment that are currently relevant for the occurrence of reinforcement.

Conditioned reinforcers

The intimate and continuing association between discriminative environmental stimulus events and the occurrence of reinforcers endows at least some stimuli that were not originally reinforcing with acquired reinforcing properties. These stimuli are called *secondary* or *conditioned reinforcers,* to distinguish them from innate, *primary* or *unconditioned reinforcers* that apparently re-

[130]

quire no experience in order to be effective. Conditioned reinforcers, like primary reinforcers, can be either *appetitive (positive)*, strengthening a prior-occurring response by their appearance, or *aversive (negative)*, strengthening a prior-occurring response by their disappearance or postponement. Under any circumstances, the development or acquisition of conditioned reinforcing properties by a stimulus is usually gradual.

Perhaps the most important aspect of the analysis of environmental stimulus events in relation to behavioral interactions is that conditioned reinforcers can gain some degree of independence from factors limiting their potency such as satiation, for example, by being associated with a wide variety of reinforcing events so that they become *generalized reinforcers*. Generalized reinforcers gain potency from all the reinforcers with which they are associated, and have broadly based discriminative and conditioned reinforcing properties. A common example of a generalized reinforcer is money.

Response chaining refers to the occurrence of a series of behaviors joined together by environmental stimuli that act both as conditioned reinforcers and as discriminative stimuli. A chain (e.g., party-going) usually begins with the occurrence of a discriminative stimulus (e.g., phone invitation) in the presence of which an appropriate response (e.g., acceptance) is followed by a conditioned reinforcer (e.g., "Glad you can make it."). This conditioned reinforcer is also the discriminative

[131]

stimulus for the next appropriate response (e.g, washing, dressing) which in turn, is followed by another conditioned reinforcer (e.g., leaving the house, catching a cab) which is also a discriminative stimulus for the next response (e.g., joining the party), and so on. While it is doubtless true that such chains are most often maintained by the intermittent terminal occurrence of potent consequences (e.g., sex, food), laboratory experiments have demonstrated that the overlapping links in the chain are also held together by the dual and demonstrably separable discriminative and conditioned reinforcing functions of the various environmental stimuli. The significance of this general chaining principle is that virtually all behavioral interactions occur as chains of greater or lesser length; even performances usually treated as unitary phenomena can be usefully analyzed as components of a response chain for purposes of modification.

Operant-respondent interactions

This overview of experimentally derived concepts and principles basic to the theory and practice of behavior therapy has thus far maintained the generally accepted differentiation between operants and respondents that is based on procedural distinctions used in the laboratory. The independent and distinctive features of these two processes are seldom apparent, however, in the course of even detailed natural observation. The complex interaction between operants and respondents is most pronounced in the experimental analysis of the aversive control procedures represented by the technical terms *escape, avoidance,* and *punishment,* and the corollary concepts of emotion and motivation.

Virtually all empirical and theoretical accounts of the behavior disorders have traditionally assigned a central role to historical and contemporary environmental interactions involving aversive stimuli. Operationally characterized in terms of their behavioral effects, aversive stimuli are defined as environmental events that increase the subsequent frequency of operant responses that remove or postpone them. When an aversive stimulus follows and is dependent on the occurrence of an operant response, a punishment condition is defined. Punishment may be made contingent on the occurrence of an operant that has never before been followed by a reinforcer, an operant currently being maintained by an appetitive (positive) or aversive (negative) reinforcer or an operant that is undergoing extinction. Under each condition, the short- and long-term effects of punishment will vary as a function of complex operant-respondent interactions, and both discriminative stimulus control and reinforcement schedule factors may influence the subsequent form and frequency of the operant behavior.

Escape occurs when a response terminates an aversive stimulus after it has appeared. The interaction between operants and respondents is especially prominent in escape situations, because the aversive stimulus usually elicits reflexive responses which eventually result in or accompany the operant escape behavior. Strong generalization effects appear during initial exposures to escape situations, but the aversive stimulus gradually develops discriminative properties. Eventually, very low intensities of the aversive stimulus may maintain an operant escape performance that had required a much more intense aversive stimulus to establish. Reinforcement schedule effects, similar in all essential respects to those associated with positive reinforcement schedules, are observed when the reinforcer is withdrawal of an aversive stimulus. Extinction of an operant escape response occurs rapidly when presentation of an aversive stimulus is discontinued, or more slowly and erratically if the formerly effective response is no longer reinforced by withdrawal of the aversive stimulus.

If an operant response postpones an aversive stimulus, it is called an *avoidance* response. Avoidance performances may be established and maintained either with or without an exteroceptive environmental event, or warning stimulus, preceding the aversive stimulus. When a warning stimulus precedes the aversive stimulus, respondent conditioning endows the warning stimulus with conditioned aversive properties, so that the operant avoidance response is reinforced by a combination of the termination of the CS (warning stimulus) and the continued absence of the aversive stimulus. Thus, in this complex avoidance process, the warning stimulus functions simultaneously as an eliciting environmental event for respondents, as a conditioned aversive (negative) reinforcer (withdrawal of which strengthens the operant avoidance performance), and as a discriminative stimulus (which sets the occasion for the operant avoidance response). In the absense of an exteroceptive warning stimulus, temporal respondent conditioning provides discriminative cues; the interoceptive temporal stimulus, correlated with the aversive environmental event, acquires the same three simultaneous functions as an exteroceptive stimulus.

This analysis of aversive control emphasizes the simultaneous operation of operant and respondent conditioning processes in ongoing behavior segments. More generally, whenever the unconditioned stimulus in a respondent conditioning procedure is also an appetitive (positive) or aversive (negative) reinforcer, operant conditioning occurs at the same time as respondent conditioning. Similarly, whenever the the reinforcer in an operant procedure is also an unconditioned stimulus, respondent conditioning proceeds at the same time as operant conditioning.

CONCLUSION

The work of the Task Force has reaffirmed our belief that behavior therapy and behavioral principles employed in the analysis of clinical phenomena have reached a stage of development where they now unquestionably have much to offer informed clinicians in the service of modern clinical and social psychiatry.

REFERENCES

1. Pavlov, I. P.: *Conditioned Reflexes.* Translated and edited by Anrep, G. V. London, Oxford University Press, 1927.
2. Pavlov, I. P.: *Lectures on Conditioned Reflexes.* Vol. I and II. Edited by Gantt, W. A. H. New York, International Publishers, 1928.
3. Bechterev, V.: *General Principles of Human Reflexology.* Translated by Murphy, E., Murphy, W. London, Hutchinson, 1932.
4. Thorndike, E. L.: *Animal intelligence—an experimental study of the associative processes in animals.* Psychol. Monogr. 2:1–106, 1898 (Monogr. suppl. whole no. 8).
5. Skinner, B. F.: *Verbal Behavior.* New York, Appleton-Century-Crofts, 1957.
6. Kintsch, W.: *Learning, Memory and Conceptual Processes.* New York, Wiley, 1970.
7. Bandura, A., Walters, R. H.: *Social Learning and Personality Development.* New York, Holt, Rinehart, and Winston, 1963.
8. Watson, J. B., Rayner, R.: *Conditioned emotional reactions.* J. Exp. Psychol. 3:1–14, 1920.
9. Jones, M. C.: *The elimination of children's fears.* J. Exp. Psychol. 7:382–390, 1924.

REFERENCES

10. Mowrer, O. H., Mowrer, W. M.: *Enuresis–a method for its study and treatment.* Am. J. Orthopsychiatry 8:436–459, 1938.
11. Ivanov-Smolensky, A. G.: *The pathology of conditioned reflexes and the so-called psychogenic depression.* J. Nerv. Ment. Dis. 67:346–350, 1928.
12. Krasnagorski, N. I.: *Physiology of cerebral activity in children as a new subject of pediatric investigation.* Am. J. Dis. Child 46:473–494, 1933.
13. Gantt, W. A. H.: *Experimental Basis for Neurotic Behavior.* New York, Harper and Brothers, 1944.
14. Liddell, H. S.: *The experimental neuroses and the problem of mental disorder.* Am. J. Psychiatry 94:1035–1043, 1938.
15. Masserman, J. H.: *Behavior and Neurosis.* Chicago, University of Chicago Press, 1943.
16. Astrup, C.: *Pavlovian Psychiatry.* Springfield, Ill., C. C. Thomas, 1965.
17. Shoben, E. J., Jr.: *Assessment of Parental Attitudes in Relation to Child Adjustment.* Provincetown, Mass., Journal Press, 1949.
18. Mowrer, O. H.: *Learning Theory and Personality Dynamics.* New York, Ronald, 1950.
19. Dollard, J., Miller, N. E.: *Personality and Psychotherapy.* New York, McGraw-Hill, 1950.
20. Wolpe, J., Lazarus, A. A.: *Behavior Therapy Techniques.* Oxford, Pergamon Press, 1966.
21. Wolpe, J.: *Psychotherapy by Reciprocal Inhibition.* Stanford, Stanford University Press, 1958.
22. Shapiro, M. B.: *An experimental approach to diagnostic psychological testing.* J. Ment. Sci. 97:748–764, 1951.
23. Shapiro, M. B.: *The single case in fundamental clinical psychological research.* Br. J. Med. Psychol. 34:255–262, 1961.

24. Eysenck, H. J.: *Discussion on the role of the psychologist in psychoanalytic practice: the psychologist as technician.* Proc. R. Soc. Med. 45:447–449, 1952.

25. Skinner, B. F.: *The Behavior of Organisms.* New York, Appleton-Century, 1938.

26. Lindsley, O. R., Skinner, B. F.: *A method for the experimental analysis of behavior of psychotic patients.* Am. Psychol. 9:419–420, 1954.

27. Ferster, C. B., DeMyer, M. K.: *The development of performances in autistic children in an automatically controlled environment.* J. Chronic Dis. 13:312–345, 1961.

28. Ayllon, T., Azrin, N.: *The measurement and reinforcement of behavior of psychotics.* J. Exp. Anal. Behav. 8:357–383, 1965.

29. Ayllon, T., Azrin, N. H.: *The Token Economy.* New York, Appleton-Century-Crofts, 1968.

30. Harris, F. R., Johnston, M. K., et al.: *Effects of positive social reinforcement on regressed crawling of a nursery school child.* J. Educ. Psychol. 55:35–41, 1964.

31. Allen, K. E., Hart, B. M., et al.: *Effects of social reinforcement on isolate behavior of a nursery school child.* Child Dev. 35:511–518, 1964.

32. Baer, D. M., Wolf, M. M.: *The reinforcement contingency in pre-school and remedial education,* in *Early Education.* Edited by Hess, R. D., Bear, R. M. Chicago, Aldine, 1968, pp. 119–129.

33. Krasner, L.: *Behavior therapy.* Annu. Rev. Psychol. 22:483–532, 1971.

34. Salzman, L.: *Psychodynamic theory and conditioning therapy.* Semin. Psychiatry 9:93–99, 1972.

35. Marmor, J. (ed.): *Modern Psychoanalysis.* New York, Basic Books, 1968.

REFERENCES

36. Lazarus, A. A.: *Phobias: broad-spectrum behavioral views.* Semin. Psychiatry 9:85–90, 1972.
37. Popper, K. R.: *The Logic of Scientific Discovery.* New York, Basic Books, 1959.
38. Skinner, B. F.: *Critique of psychoanalytic concepts and theories.* The Sci. Monthly 79:300–305, 1954.
39. Hilgard, E. R.: *Experimental approaches to psychoanalysis,* in *Psychoanalysis as Science.* Edited by Pumpian-Mindlin, E. New York, Basic Books, 1952, pp. 3–45.
40. Rado, S.: *Psychoanalysis of Behavior.* Vol. I. New York: Grune and Stratton, 1956.
41. Bieber, I.: *A critique of the libido theory.* Am. J. Psychoanal. 18:52–68, 1958. .
42. Marmor, J.: *New directions in psychoanalytic theory and therapy,* in *Modern Psychoanalysis.* Edited by Marmor, J. New York, Basic Books, 1968, pp. 3–15.
43. Glover, E.: *Freud or Jung.* New York, Norton, 1950.
44. Pumpian-Mindlin, E.: *The position of psychoanalysis in relation to the biological and social sciences,* in *Psychoanalysis as Science.* Edited by Pumpian-Mindlin, E. New York, Basic Books, 1952, pp. 125–158.
45. Grinker, R. R., Sr.: *Conceptual progress in psychoanalysis,* in *Modern Psychoanalysis.* Edited by Marmor, J. New York, Basic Books, 1968, pp. 19–43.
46. Kubie, L. S.: *Missing and wanted: heterodoxy in psychiatry and psychoanalysis.* J. Nerv. Ment. Dis. 137:311, 1963.
47. Birk, L.: *Behavior therapy—integration with dynamic psychiatry.* Behav. Ther. 1:522–526 1970.
48. Feather, B. W., Rhoads, J. M.: *Psychodynamic behavior therapy: I. theory and rationale.* Arch. Gen. Psychiatry 26:496–502, 1972.
49. Marmor, J.: *Dynamic psychotherapy and behavior therapy.* Arch. Gen. Psychiatry 24:22–28, 1971.

50. Crisp, A. H.: *'Transference', 'symptom emergence' and 'social repercussion' in behavior therapy: a study of fifty-four treated patients.* Br. J. Med. Psychol. 39:179–196, 1966.

51. Salter, A.: *Conditioned Reflex Therapy.* New York, Farrar, Straus, 1949.

52. Brady, J. P.: *Brevital-relaxation treatment of frigidity.* Behav. Res. Ther. 4:71–77, 1966.

53. Jacobson, E.: *Progressive Relaxation.* Chicago, University of Chicago Press, 1938.

54. Lazarus, A. A., Rachman, S.: *The use of systematic desensitization in psychotherapy.* S. Afr. Med. J. 31:934–937, 1957.

55. Lazovik, A. D., Lang, P. J.: *A laboratory demonstration of systematic desensitization psychotherapy.* J. Psycho. Stud. 11:238–247, 1960.

56. Lazarus, A. A.: *Group therapy of phobic disorders by systematic desensitization.* J. Abnorm. Soc. Psychol. 63:504–510, 1961.

57. Lazarus, A. A.: *The treatment of chronic frigidity by systematic desensitization.* J. Nerv. Ment. Dis. 136:272–278, 1963.

58. Geer, J. H., Katkin, E. S.: *Treatment of insomnia using a variant of systematic desensitization: a case report.* J. Abnorm. Psychol. 71:161–164, 1966.

59. Bond, I. K., Hutchinson, H. C.: *Application of reciprocal inhibition therapy to exhibitionism.* Can. Med. Assoc. J. 83:23–25, 1960.

60. Friedman, D.: *A new technique for the systematic desensitization of phobic symptoms.* Behav. Res. Ther. 4:139–140, 1966.

61. Lazarus, A. A., Abramovitz, A.: *The use of "emotive imagery" in the treatment of children's phobias.* J. Ment. Sci. 108:191–195, 1962.

REFERENCES

62. Paul, G. L.: *Outcome of systematic desensitization: II. Controlled investigation of individual treatment, technique variations, and current status,* in *Behavior Therapy.* Edited by Franks, C. M. New York, McGraw-Hill, 1969, pp. 105–159.

63. Marks, I. M.: *Fears and Phobias.* London, Academic Press, 1969.

64. Bernstein, D. A., Paul, G. L.: *Some comments on therapy analogue research with small animal "phobias."* J. Behav. Ther. Exp. Psychiatry 2:225–237, 1971.

65. Lazarus, A. A., Serber, M.: *Is systematic desensitization being misapplied.* Psychol. Rep. 23:215–218, 1968.

66. Lang, P. J.: *The mechanics of desensitization and the laboratory study of human fear,* in *Behavior Therapy.* Edited by Franks, C. M. New York, McGraw-Hill, 1969, pp. 160–191.

67. Ayllon, T.: *Toward a new hospital psychiatry,* in *The New Hospital Psychiatry.* Edited by Abrams, G., Greenfield, N. New York, Academic Press, 1971, pp. 275–287.

68. Ayllon, T., Roberts, M.: *The token economy: now!* in *Behavior Modification.* Edited by Agras, W. S., Boston, Little, Brown and Co. (in press).

69. Gelfand, D. M., Gelfand, S., Dobson, W. R.: *Unprogrammed reinforcement of patients' behavior in a mental hospital.* Behav. Res. Ther. 5:201–207, 1967.

70. Ayllon, T., Haughton, E.: *Modification of systematic verbal behavior of mental patients.* Behav. Res. Ther. 2:87–97, 1964.

71. Paul, G. L.: *Chronic mental patients: current status—future directions.* Psychol. Bull. 71:81–94, 1969.

72. Anderson, R. C.: *Educational psychology.* Annu. Rev. Psychol. 18:129–164, 1967.

73. O'Leary, K. D., Drabman, R.: *Token reinforcement programs in the classroom: a review.* Psychol. Bull. 75:379–398, 1971.

74. Cohen, H. L., Filipczak, J.: *A New Learning Environment.* San Francisco, Jossey-Bass, 1971.

75. Boren, J. J., Colman, A. D.: *Some experiments on reinforcement principles within a psychiatric ward for delinquent soliders.* J. Appl. Behav. Anal. 3:29–37, 1970.

76. Colman, A. D.: *Planned Environment in Psychiatric Treatment.* Springfield, Ill., C. C. Thomas, 1971.

77. Minge, M. R., Ball, T. S.: *Teaching of self-help skills to profoundly retarded patients.* Am. J. Ment. Defic. 71:864–868, 1967.

78. Zimmerman, E. H., Zimmerman, J., Russell, C. D.: *Differential effects of token reinforcement on instruction-following behavior in retarded students instructed as a group.* J. Appl. Behav. Anal. 2:101–112, 1969.

79. O'Leary, K. D., Poulos, R. W., Devine, V. T.: *Tangible reinforcers: bonuses or bribes?* J. Consult. Clin. Psychol. 38:1–8, 1972.

80. Ferster, C. B.: *Clinical reinforcement.* Semin. Psychiatry 9:101–111, 1972.

81. Max, L. W.: *Breaking up a homosexual fixation by the conditioned reaction technique: a case study.* Psychol. Bull. 32:734, 1935.

82. Raymond, M.: *Case of fetishism treated by aversion therapy.* Br. Med. J. 2:854–857, 1956.

83. Feldman, M. P., MacCulloch, M. J.: *A systematic approach to the treatment of homosexuality by conditioned aversion: preliminary report.* Am. J. Psychiatry 121:167–172, 1964.

84. Feldman, M. P., MacCulloch, M. J.: *The application of*

REFERENCES

anticipatory-avoidance learning to the treatment of homosexuality: I. theory, technique and preliminary results. Behav. Res. Ther. 2:165–183, 1965.

85. Feldman, M. P., MacCulloch, M. J.: *Homosexual Behavior: Therapy and Assessment.* Oxford, Pergamon Press, 1971.

86. Birk, L., Miller, E. Cohler, B.: *Group psychotherapy for homosexual men by male-female cotherapists.* Acta Psychiatrica Scandinavica, Special Supplement, 218, 1970.

87. Voegtlin, W. L., Lemere, F.: *The treatment of alcohol addiction: a review of the literature.* J. Stud. Alcohol 2:717–803, 1942.

88. Lovibond, S. H.: *Aversive control of behavior.* Behav. Ther. 1:80–91, 1970.

89. Risley, T. R.: *The effects and side effects of punishing the autistic behaviors of a deviant child.* J. Appl. Behav. Anal. 1:21–34, 1968.

90. Lovaas, O. I., Freitag, G., et al.: *A recording method and observations of behaviors of normal and autistic children in free play settings.* J. Exp. Child Psychol. 1:99–109, 1965.

91. Bucher, B., Lovaas, O. I.: *Use of aversive stimulation in behavior modification, in Miami Symposium on the Prediction of Behavior, 1967.* Edited by Jones, M. R. Coral Gables, University of Miami Press, 1968, pp. 77–145.

92. Sears, R. R., Maccoby, E., Levin H.: *Patterns of Child-Rearing.* Evanston, Ill., Row, Peterson, 1957.

93. Bandura, A.: *Principles of Behavior Modification.* New York, Holt, Rinehart and Winston, 1969.

94. Gardner, W. I.: *Use of punishment procedures with the severely retarded: a review.* Am. J. Ment. Defic. 74:86–103, 1969.

95. Azrin, N. H., Holz, W. C.: *Punishment in Operant*

Behavior. Edited by Honig, W. K. New York, Appleton-Century-Crofts, 1966, pp. 380–447.

96. Church, R. M.: *The varied effects of punishment on behavior.* Psychol. Rev. 70:369–402, 1963.

97. Solomon, R. L.: *Punishment.* Am. Psychol. 19:239–253, 1964.

98. Lazarus, A. A.: *Behavior Therapy and Beyond.* New York, McGraw-Hill, 1971.

99. Fehr, F. S., Stern, J. A.: *Peripheral physiological variables and emotion: The James-Lange theory revisited.* Psychol. Bull. 74:411–424, 1970.

100. Liberman, R. P.: *Behavioral methods in group and family therapy.* Semin. Psychiatry, 9:145–156, 1972.

101. Lomont, J. F., Gilner, F. H., et al.: *Group assertion training and group insight therapies.* Psychol. Rep. 25:463–470, 1969.

102. Hedquist, F. J., Weinhold, B. K.: *Behavioral group counseling with socially anxious and unassertive college students.* J. Counseling Psychol. 17:237–242, 1970.

103. Guttmacher, J., Birk, L.: *Group therapy: can it be the treatment of choice?* Comprehensive Psychiatry, 12:1971.

104. Bandura, A.: *Psychotherapy based upon modeling principles, in Handbook of Psychotherapy and Behavior Change.* Edited by Bergin, A. E., Garfield, S. L. New York, Wiley, 1971, pp. 653–708.

105. Ellis, A.: *Reason and Emotion in Psychotherapy.* New York, Lyle Stuart, 1962.

106. Baum, M.: *Extinction of avoidance responding through response prevention (flooding).* Psychol. Bull. 74:276–284, 1970.

107. Boulougouris, J. C., Marks, I. M., Marset, P.: *Superiority*

of flooding (implosion) to desensitization for reducing pathological fear. Behav. Res. Ther. 9:7–16, 1971.

108. Mealiea, W. L., Jr., Nawas, M. M.: *The comparative effectiveness of systematic desensitization and implosive therapy in the treatment of snake phobia.* J. Behav. Ther. Exp. Psychiatry, 2:85–94, 1971.

109. Marks, I.: *Perspective on flooding.* Semin. Psychiatry, 9:129–138, 1972.

110. Brady, J. P.: *Metronome-conditioned speech retraining for stuttering.* Behav. Ther. 2:129–150, 1971.

111. Barber, V.: *Studies in the psychology of stuttering:* XVI. *rhythm as a distraction in stuttering.* J. Speech Hear. Disord. 5:29–42, 1940.

112. Meyer, V., Mair, J. M. M.: *A new technique to control stammering: a preliminary report.* Behav. Res. Ther. 1:251–254, 1963.

113. Brady, J. P.: *Studies on the metronome effect on stuttering.* Behav. Res. Ther. 7:197–204, 1969.

114. Jones, R. J., Azrin, N. H.: *Behavioral engineering: stuttering as a function of stimulus duration during speech synchronization.* J. Appl. Behav. Anal. 2:223–229, 1969.

115. Yates, A. J.: *Behavior Therapy.* New York, Wiley, 1970.

116. Frederick, C. J.: *Treatment of a tic by systematic desensitization and massed response evocation.* J. Behav. Ther. Exp. Psychiatry 2:281–283, 1971.

117. Truax, C. B.: *Reinforcement and non-reinforcement in Rogerian psychotherapy.* J. Abnorm. Psychol. 71:1–9, 1966.

118. Shapiro, D., Birk, L.: *Group therapy in experimental perspective.* Int. J. Group Psychother. 17:211–224, 1967.

119. Alexander, F.: *The dynamics of psychotherapy in the light of learning theory.* Am. J. Psychiatry 120:441–448, 1963.

120. Baker, B.L.: *Symptom treatment and symptom substitution in enuresis.* J. Abnorm. Psychol. 74:42–49, 1969.

121. Ullman, L., Krasner, L.: *Introduction,* in *Case Studies in Behavior Modification.* Edited by Ullmann, L., Krasner, L. New York, Holt, Rinehart and Winston, 1965, pp. 1–63.

122. Buell, J., Stoddard, P., et al.: *Collateral social development accompanying reinforcement of outdoor play in a preschool child.* J. Appl. Behav. Anal. 1:167–173, 1968.

123. Rubin, B. K., Stolz, S. B.: *Generalization of self-referent speech established in a retarded adolescent by operant procedures.* Behav. Ther. (in press).

124. Budzynski, T. H., Stoyva, J. M., Adler, C. S.: *Feedback-induced muscle relaxation: application to tension headache.* J. Behav. Ther. Exp.. Psychiatry 1:205–211, 1970.

125. Razran, G.: *The observable unconscious and the inferable conscious in current Soviet psychophysiology: interoceptive conditioning, semantic conditioning, and the orienting reflex.* Psychol. Rev. 68:81–147, 1961.

126. Harlow, H. F.: *From thought to therapy: lessons from a primate laboratory.* Amer. Scientest 59:538–549, 1971.

127. Gantt, W. H.: *Cardiovascular component of the conditional reflex to pain, food and other stimuli.* Physiol. Rev. 40:266–291, 1960.

128. Gantt, W. H., Newton, J. E. O., Royer, F. L., Stephens, J. H.: *Effects of person.* Cond. Reflex 1:18–35, 1966.

129. Anderson, Gantt, W. H.: *The effect of person on cardiac and motor responsivity to shock in dogs.* Cond. Reflex 1:181–189, 1966.

130. Lynch, J. J., McCarthy, J. F.: *The effect of petting on a classically conditioned emotional response.* Behav. Res. Ther, 5:55–62, 1967.

REFERENCES

131. Murphee, O. D., Dykman, R. A., Peters, J. E.: *Operant conditioning of two strains of pointer dogs.* Psychophysiology 3:414–417, 1967.
132. Newton, J. E. O., Ehrlich, W.: *Coronary blood flow in dogs: effect of person.* Cond. Reflex 4:81–88, 1969.
133. Lynch, J. J., McCarthy, J. F.: *Social responding in dogs: heart rate changes to a person.* Psychophysiology 5:389–393, 1969.
134. Lynch, J. J.: *Psychophysiology and development of social attachment.* J. Neru. Ment. Dis. 151:231–244, 1970.
135. Hunter, M.: *The effects of interpersonal interaction upon the task performance of chronic schizophrenics.* Unpublished doctoral dissertation, Columbia University, 1961.
136. Fisher, E. H.: *Task performance of chronic schizophrenics as a function of verbal evaluation and social proximity.* J. Clin. Psychol. 19:176–178, 1963.
137. Gelburd, A. S., Anker, J. M.: *Humans as reinforcing stimuli in schizophrenic performance.* J. Abnorm. Psychol. 75:795–798, 1970.
138. Gattozzi, R. E.: *The effect of person on a conditioned emotional response of schizophrenic and normal subjects.* Cond. Reflex 6:181–190, 1971.
139. Thomas, E. J., Abrams, K. S., Johnson, J. B.: *Self-monitoring and reciprocal inhibition in the modification of multiple tics of Gilles de la Tourette's syndrome.* J. Behav. Ther. Exp. Psychiatry 2:159–171, 1971.
140. Browning, R. M., Stover, D. O.: *Behavior Modification in Child Treatment.* Chicago, Aldine-Atherton, 1971.
141. Sanderson, R., Campbell, D., LaVerty, S.: *An investigation of a new aversive conditioning treatment for alcoholism, in Conditioning Techniques in Clinical Practice and Research.* Edited by Franks, C. M. New York, Springer, 1964, pp. 165–177.

142. Forel, A.: *Der Hypnotismus*. Stuttgart, Germany, von Ferdinand Enke, 1902.

143. Wolf, S.: *Effects of suggestion and conditioning on the action of chemical agents in human subjects*. J. Clin. Invest. 29:100–109, 1950.

144. Rosenthal, R.: *Experimenter Effects in Behavioral Research*. New York, Appleton-Century-Crofts, 1966.

145. Kale, R. J., Kaye, J. H., et al.: *The effects of reinforcement on the modification, maintenance and generalization of social responses of mental patients*. J. Appl. Behav. Anal. 1:307–314, 1968.

146. Ullmann, L. P., Krasner, L. (eds.): *Case Studies in Behavior Modification*. New York, Holt, Rinehart, and Winston, 1965.

147. Thompson, T., Grabowski, J. (eds.): *Behavior Modification of the Mentally Retarded*. New York, Oxford University Press. 1972.

148. Baer, D., Wolf, M. M., Risley, T.: *Some current dimensions of applied behavior analysis*. J. Appl. Behav. Anal. 1:91–97, 1968.

149. Liberman, R. P., Smith, V.: *A multiple baseline study of systematic desensitization in a patient with multiple phobias*. Behav. Ther. 3:597–603, 1972.

150. Paul, G. L.: *Insight Versus Desensitization in Psychotherapy*. Stanford, Stanford University Press, 1966.

151. Paul, G. L.: *Insight versus desensitization in psychotherapy two years after termination*. J. Consult, Psychol. 31:333–348, 1967.

152. Gelder, M. G., Marks, I. M., Wolff, H. H.: *Desensitization and psychotherapy in the treatment of phobic states: a controlled inquiry*. Br. J. Psychiatry 113:53–73, 1967.

REFERENCES

153. Gelder, M. G., Marks, I. M.: *Desensitization and phobias: a cross-over study.* Br. J. Psychiatry 114:323–328, 1968.
154. Grossberg. J. M.: *Behavior therapy: a review.* Psychol. Bull. 62:73–88, 1964.
155. Leff, R.: *Behavior modification and the psychoses of childhood: a review.* Psychol. Bull. 69:396–409, 1968.
156. Greenspoon, J.: *The reinforcing effect of two spoken sounds on the frequency of two responses.* Am. J. Psychol. 68:409–416, 1955.
157. Frank, J. D.: *Persuasion and Healing.* Baltimore, Johns Hopkins Press, 1961.
158. Birk, L.: *Case report: social reinforcement in psychotherapy.* Cond. Reflex 3:116–123, 1968.
159. Liberman, R.: *Behavioral approaches to family and couple therapy.* Am. J. Orthopsychiatry 40:106–118, 1970.
160. Wolpe, J.: *Psychotherapy by reciprocal inhibition: a reply to Dr. Glover.* Br. J. Med. Psychol. 32:232–235, 1959.
161. Brady, J. P.: *Brevital-aided systematic desensitization,* in *Advances in Behavior Therapy, 1969.* Edited by Rubin, R. D., Fensterheim, H., et al., New York, Academic Press, 1971, pp. 77–83.
162. Birk, L., Huddleston, W., et al.: *Avoidance conditioning for homosexuality.* Arch. Gen. Psychiatry 25:314–323, 1971.
163. Bancroft, J.: *Homosexuality: a pilot study of 10 cases.* Br. J. Psychiatry 115:1417–1431, 1969.
164. Masters, W. H., Johnson, V. E.: *Human Sexual Inadequacy.* New York, Norton, 1971.
165. Henderson, A. S., Montgomery, I. M., Williams, C. L.: *Psychological immunization: a proposal for preventive psychiatry.* Lancet 1:1111–1113, 1972.
166. Patterson, G. R., Gullion, M. E.: *Living with Children.* Champaign, Ill., Research Press, 1968.

167. Smith, J. M., Smith, D. E. P.: *Child Management*. Ann Arbor, Ann Arbor Publishers, 1966.

168. Becker, W. C.: *Parents are Teachers*. Champaign, Ill., Research Press, 1971.

169. Becker, W. C., Thomas, D. R., Carnive, D.: *Reducing Behavior Problems* (in *The State of the Art series*). Urbana, Ill., University of Illinois Educational Resource Information Center, Dec. 1969.

170. Buckley, N. K., Walker, H. M.: *Modifying Classroom Behavior*. Champaign, Ill., Research Press, 1970.

171. McAllister, L. W., Stachowiak, J. G., et al.: *The application of operant conditioning techniques in a secondary school classroom*. J. Appl. Behav. Anal. 2:277–285, 1969.

172. Stuart, R. B.: *Behavioral control of delinquency: critique of existing programs and recommendations for innovative programming*, in *Behavior Modification for Exceptional Children and Youth*. Edited by Hamerlynck, L. A., Clark, F. C. Calgary, Alberta, University of Calgary, 1971, pp. 97–128.

173. Ayllon, T., Michael, J.: *The psychiatric nurse as a behavioral engineer*. J. Exp. Anal. Behav. 2:323–334, 1959.

174. O'Leary, K. D.: *The entrée of the paraprofessional into the classroom*, in *Behavior Modification: Issues and Extensions*. Edited by Bijon, S. W., Ribes-Inesta, E. New York, Academic Press (in press).

175. Zeilberger, J., Sampen, S. E., Sloane, H. N., Jr.: *Modification of a child's problem behaviors in the home with the mother as therapist*. J. Appl. Behav. Anal. 1:47–53, 1968.

176. Laws, D. R., Brown, R. A., et al.: *Reduction of inappropriate social behavior in disturbed children by an untrained*

paraprofessional therapist. Behav. Ther. 2:519–533, 1971.

177. Staats, A. W., Minke, K. A., Butts, P. A.: *A token-reinforcement remedial reading program administered by black therapy-technicians to problem black children.* Behav. Ther. 1:331–353, 1970.

178. Winett, R. A., Winkler, R. C.: *Current behavior modification in the classroom: be still, be quiet, be docile.* J. Appl. Behav. Anal. 5:499–504, 1972.

179. Agras, W. S., *Covert conditioning.* Semin. Psychiatry 9:157–163, 1972.

180. Stampfl, T. G., Lewis, D. J.: *Essentials of implosive therapy: a learning-theory-based psychodynamic behavioral therapy.* J. Abnorm. Psychol. 72:496–503, 1967.

181. Baum, M., Poser, E. G.: *Comparison of flooding procedures in animals and men.* Behav. Res. Ther. 9:249–254, 1971.

182. Seligman, M. E. P., Maier, S. F., Solomon, R. L.: *Unpredictable and uncontrollable aversive events,* in *Aversive Conditioning and Learning.* Edited by Brush, F. R. New York, Academic Press, 1971, pp. 347–400.

183. Stolerman, I. P., Kumar, R.: *Preferences for morphine in rats: validation of and experimental model of dependence.* Psychopharmacologia 17:137–150, 1970.

184. Brady, J. P., Lind, D. L.: *Experimental analysis of hysterical blindness: operant conditioning techniques.* Arch. Gen. Psychiatry 4:331–339, 1961.

185. Stolz, S. B., Wolf, M. M.: *Visually disriminated behavior in a "blind" adolescent retardate.* J. Appl. Behav. Anal. 2:65–77, 1969.

186. Walton, D., Mather, M. D.: *The application of learning principles to the treatment of obsessive-compulsive states in the acute and chronic phases of illness,* in *Experiments in Be-*

havior Therapy. Edited by Eysenck, H. J. New York, Macmillan, 1964, pp. 117–151.

187. Azrin, N. H., Powell, J.: *Behavioral engineering: the reduction of smoking behavior by a conditioning apparatus and procedure.* J. Appl. Behav. Anal. 1:193–200, 1968.

188. Thomas, E. J., Carter, R. D., et al.: *A signal system for the assessment and modification of behavior (SAM).* Behav. Ther. 1:252–259, 1970.

189. Brady, J. P.: *Drugs in behavior therapy,* in *Psychopharmacology: A Review of Progress, 1957—1967.* Edited by Efron, D. H. Public Health Service Publication no. 1836. Washington, D.C., U.S. Government Printing Office, 1968, pp. 271–280.

190. Silverstone, T.: *The use of drugs in behavior therapy.* Behav. Ther. 1:485–497, 1970.

191. Benson, H., Shapiro, D., et al.: *Decreased systolic blood pressure through operant conditioning techniques in patients with essential hypertension.* Science 173:740–742, 1971.

192. Surwit, R. S.: *Biofeedback: A possible treatment for Reynaud's disease,* in *Behavioral Medicine: The Use of Biofeedback Training in Psychosomatic Disorders.* New York, Grune and Stratton, (in press).

193. Weiss, T., Engel, B. T.: *Operant conditioning of heart rate in patients with premature ventricular contractions.* Psychosom. Med. 33:301–321, 1971.

194. Lutker, E. R.: *Treatment of migraine headache by conditioned relaxation: a case study.* Behav. Ther. 2:592–593, 1971.

195. Green, E., Green, A., Sargent, J., Walters, D.: *Biofeedback for tension and migraine headache,* in *Behavioral Medicine: The Use of Biofeedback Training in Psychosomatic Disorders.* New York, Grune and Stratton, (in press).

REFERENCES

196. Yen, S.: *Survey of courses in behavior modification at higher learning institutions.* Presented at the 5th Annual Meeting of Association for Advancement of Behavior Therapy, Washington, D.C., Sept. 5–6, 1971.

197. Brady, J. P.: *The place of behavior therapy in medical student and psychiatric resident training: two surveys and some recommendations.* J. Nerv. Ment. Dis. (in press).

198. Poser, E. G.: *Training behavior therapists.* Behav. Res. Ther. 5:37–41, 1967.

199. Houts, P. S.: *Individualized instruction in behavior therapy for medical students.* Presented at the 5th Annual Meeting of Association for Advancement of Behavior Therapy, Washington, D.C., Sept. 5–6, 1971.

200. Gelfand, S.: *A behavior modification program for psychiatric residents.* J. Behav. Ther. Exp. Psychiatry 3:147–152, 1972.

201. Edward, N. B.: *Behavior therapy training in the United States.* J. Behav. Ther. Exp. Psychiatry 1:179–181, 1970.